RISE ABOVE

Surviving Depression and
Living a Better Life

by

JOHN MELNICK

HI ELAINE,   AUG 2023
THANKS FOR YOUR INTEREST
AND SUPPORT
   TO YOUR MENTAL HEALTH
RISE ABOVE

John Melnick
X

A Wood Dragon Book

RISE ABOVE - Surviving Depression and Living a Better Life

Cover design: Callum Jagger
Author photos: Carlene Clark
Interior design: Christine Lee

Published by:
Wood Dragon Books
Post Office Box 429
Mossbank, Saskatchewan, Canada S0H3G0
www.wooddragonbooks.com

ISBN: 978-1-990863-11-0 Paperback
ISBN: 978-1-990863-19-6 Hardcover
ISBN: 978-1-990863-12-7 eBook

To contact the author:
www.JohnMelnick.ca
Email: info@johnmelnick.ca

TABLE OF CONTENTS

DEDICATION

To Dr. Don Rodgers, my Godfather and friend.
Don was a Psychiatrist who dedicated his life
to help improve Mental Health services
in Manitoba and Northern Canada.
"Uncle Don," as I called him,
was wonderfully helpful in getting me
through the worst days of my depression
and on track to live a healthier, happier life.

DISCLAIMER

This is my story of growth and learning while living with depression. Out of respect for the many people who have crossed paths with me, some names have been changed to protect their privacy. The names of my family members are real.

My parents loved me and did their best to raise their children. Through healing eyes, I better understand my father who, over time, reflected on his actions in the past. He opened his mind to the possibilities that his actions created significant challenges for those he loved. I am grateful that he apologized to me when I was in recovery. His apology freed me from blaming myself for things that I was not responsible for. I now walk away from people who try to blame me for the consequences of their actions by using guilt. I now live my life on my terms, being responsible for my own actions, but not the actions of others. My mother, unfortunately, was never able to do what my father did, opening herself up to learning new approaches to life.

INTRODUCTION

I suffer from mental illness. The disease gradually consumed me, taking over my mind to the point where I calmly walked into a river, prepared to end my life. I survived what I call my *suicide attack* and was left with a sense of purpose and calling.

We need to talk about mental health and permanently erase any stigma or embarrassment attached to it. Like all people with life-altering diseases, we who experience depression are unique in personalities and circumstances - but the anguish, the pain, the hopelessness and the struggles in the shadows of depression are common to us all. Anyone who gets to the point of dangerous, artificial calm after the pain desperately needs help. I survived the artificial calm with a new sense of purpose and a drive to educate others about mental health. I also hope to inspire people to talk about mental health and share their stories. It is through sharing that we can heal, move on, and continue to help others.

Mental illness affects 1 in 5 people in Canada. By the age of 40, approximately 50% of the population will have experienced some form of mental illness. Major depression affects approximately 5.4% of the Canadian population, and anxiety disorders affect 4.6% of the population.[1]

4,012 Canadians died by suicide in 2019.[2] The mortality rate due to suicide among men is three times the rate among women.[3] The economic cost of mental illnesses to the Canadian healthcare and social support system was projected as $79.9 billion for the year 2021.[4]

I am grateful to the medical experts, colleagues, friends, loved ones and especially my wife Jan who helped me deal with mental illness at various points in my life. Without their support and some hard work of my own, I would not have lived to help and encourage others. This is my story.

---

(1) https://www150.statcan.gc.ca/n1/pub/82-003-x/2020012/article/00002-eng.htm
(2) https://www150.statcan.gc.ca/t1/tbl1/en/tv.action?pid=1310039401
(3) https://www.canada.ca/en/public-health/services/publications/healthy-living/suicide-canada-key-statistics-infographic.html
(4) https://www.mentalhealthcommission.ca/sites/default/files/2016-06/Investing_in_Mental_Health_FINAL_Version_ENG.pdf

BASEBALL

I love baseball. I love it as a player and as a fan.

I love the game so much that when minor league baseball re-established itself in Winnipeg in the mid-1990s after a 35-year absence, I was the first person to sign up for season tickets. A day at the ball park is like heaven to me.

As I drive closer to the stadium, the anticipation of a game grows. More and more cars join the bumper-to-bumper procession heading for our common destination and as we get closer to the field, we funnel into the parking lots nearby. Full of fun and excitement, young children jump out of vehicles. Many carry their gloves in hope of catching an elusive fly ball hit up into the stands … even better if it's a home run ball.

Outside the stadium, staff call out, "Get your programs here." I wonder how they do it and not have hoarse voices by the time they pack up for the day.

Once inside, I inhale the smells of hot dogs, popcorn, fresh pretzels, hamburgers, and cabbage rolls. Yes, cabbage rolls. After all, it's Winnipeg, Manitoba on the Canadian Prairies. Each game, I head over to my regular food vendor stop.

"The best food stop in the ball park. How's business today?" I ask.

"Better now that our best customer, the Pickle Man, is here."

"I'll have the biggest pickle in the jar." I smile and give the staff a wink.

"Yeah, yeah. Of course, you will. Opened a fresh jar just for you."

"Bet you say that to all your customers."

Our banter is familiar and comfortable like a well-worn baseball glove that has been broken in just right.

Walking out from underneath the stands to my seat, I see the trickle of fans gradually filling the stadium. I always arrive early to watch the warm ups and soak up the atmosphere. As I walk to my seat, the cement floor is still free of the debris soon to follow as fans munch their way along with the excitement of the game. If I leave my seat in the 7th inning stretch for more snacks or a trip to the washroom, I won't mind doing the peanut shell shuffle stomp across the crunchy carpet. After all, what is a ballgame without food?

As I settle in, I happily converse with people around me as they start to arrive.

"How will our team do today?"

"Beautiful day for baseball."

"How well do you think the team is warming up today?"

No one can be bored at a game. On the field, our mascots, Goldie and Goldette, are always bubbly and entertaining in their bright yellow attire and up on the big screen, the team's Goldeye logo dances between scans of the crowd. But for the more serious fans like me, we like to watch the large screen, not for glimpses of whether we appear in crowd shots but for all the statistics that flash on the scoreboard. When it comes to baseball stats, I happily become a pseudo mathematician and there's no better sport for statistics than baseball.

Once the game starts, there's the familiar smack of a ball in a glove, the crack of the bat hitting the ball and the roar of the crowd that follows. We watch with anticipation every slide into home plate and wait to hear the umpire call out "safe" or "out" with gestures to match. Yes, this is heaven.

Besides entertainment alone, I have my own take on how I watch the game. I study the pitcher and how his arm moves. I predict whether he'll throw a fast ball or a curve ball and how he will try to throw the batter off his game. Baseball has always been a major part of my life. I was inducted into the Manitoba Baseball Hall of Fame in 2015. It was one of the proudest moments of my life. I love to share insights into the strategies the managers and players of the teams are using. So, I'm sure you're not surprised that I often get asked by friends and colleagues, "Can I watch the game with you, John?"

Baseball was something that was mine. I could do it on my own. My father always wanted to oversee things and tell me what to do. His constant need to control and micromanage led me to feel incompetent. But he knew nothing about the game of baseball, so he couldn't tell me how to play. Baseball was a place where I received a lot of respect and forged many friendships. At many tournaments where my team played and lost out early, other teams would often ask me to pitch for them. They even paid me for my services. It felt wonderful to be successful and appreciated.

The first championship team that I played on was when I was age 12 with the Greendell Community Club in the St. Vital Little League. We won the city title. In 1973, when I was 21, I played with the Norwood St. Boniface Legionnaires, a team in the Manitoba Junior Baseball League. In the final series, we played the team from Carman, Manitoba (about 40 minutes southwest of Winnipeg). As a pitcher, I had never beaten Carman in all the years that I was in the junior league. But that year, I did. I actually ended the year undefeated at 10-0. I beat them twice, once during the season and then again when we won the provincial championship 4 games to 1. This boosted my confidence. *The feeling of I can succeed at something without my father* was very important.

After the championship game and the on-field celebration of clinching the pennant, we went back to the legion hall.

Norwood St. Boniface Legion Hall was our team sponsor and we were happy to celebrate alongside the members with a few beers and lot of chatter. We were in our early 20s and I often reflect on our responsibility-free life compared to these veterans who spent their 20s defeating Hitler. Early into the evening, our Coach Jim approached me. He had been presented with the championship trophy. He put it on the table beside where I was sitting.

"John, I want you to take this home first because no one did more for us than you ... for us to win this title."

I was speechless. I didn't know what to say. I've always been one to say that we win as a team. And yet when another pitcher has a success, I congratulate him as a pitcher because I know what it takes and how it works. I've since learned how to be much better at accepting thanks or praise instead of deflecting it. But at that time, I just didn't know what to say. I think I actually teared up.

Usually, I'm right in the middle of the conversation, chiming in and cracking jokes. That night I was quiet. One of the other coaches, Coach Steve noticed and came up to me.

"John, you're very quiet, it's just not like you."

"Steve, we did all our talking on the field. I'm just absorbing this moment. I don't have anything more to say."

After that memorable year, I switched to the senior league and played until 1978. I had a good first half of the season in 1978. Then I hurt my shoulder. I remember it distinctly. I threw a pitch and I felt and heard a pop. I knew something was wrong. However, I didn't know the extent of the injury and I kept playing. Like most athletes, I was sore, but I expected the soreness to go away. This time it was different. After that pitch when I felt and heard the pop, my control of my pitches disappeared. When I threw the ball with my regular arm action, it wouldn't go where I expected it to go. Only if I slowed the velocity of my pitch, could I control the ball's direction.

Towards the end of the summer of 1978, two tournaments were held—one in Carberry, Manitoba and the other in Giroux, Manitoba. The winners of the two tournaments would play off for the right to represent Manitoba at the Western Canadian championship tournament to be held in Nanaimo, B.C. Because my pitching was suspect, I wasn't initially asked to be on the all-star team that played in Carberry. However, the team needed a full roster of twenty-five names, so the coaches asked if they could add my name to their roster. I ended up playing for the team and I won two nine-inning ball games as a pitcher. We won the Carberry tournament, qualifying us to play off the Giroux tournament winner from Carman. If we wouldn't have won those two games, we wouldn't have gone on to the next level, winning against Carman for the Manitoba title and qualifying our team to go on to Nanaimo, B.C. to play for the Western Canadian Championship. We won the Western Canadian title and I pitched through it all with a shoulder injury.

After the trip to B.C., I went to a sports doctor and asked him what was going on with my shoulder.

"John, do you think that you will ever make a living playing baseball? he asked.

"No. If it hasn't happened, it won't. A scout would have

noticed me 8-10 years ago if I would have had a chance."

"You have a torn rotator cuff. Even after surgery, your throwing arm will never be the same. I wouldn't recommend surgery, unless you have big hopes for professional playing."

And with that, I went from a player to a spectator, a pitcher to a fan.

When I go into organizations to tell my story, I get asked how traumatic it was that the injury ended my ability to play baseball. It wasn't traumatic. I have to say that I was very matter-of-fact about the change. I couldn't play anymore, but there would be other ways to enjoy my favourite game. The adjustment from playing to being a spectator was a non-issue. I had always been a spectator and a student of the game. The Winnipeg Goldeyes were 18 years away from starting up, but I attended the odd local junior game and involved myself in an MLB fantasy draft. We took turns choosing players we wanted on our individual rosters and at the end of the year, the person with the most points won the pool. I won the pool my first year, no doubt thanks to the considerable research I completed on the players and my own background.

As I and my fellow ball players aged out of playing, many of us made the transition to golf. The sport may have changed but the people in my life did not. The game ended up being a lesson in maintaining a good balance in my life. Golf opened up a whole new area of enjoyment for me.

When the Goldeyes started in Winnipeg in the mid-1990s, I encouraged my business partner to join me in going to the ball park. Watching baseball live is different than football or hockey.

We were both networkers and loved the social activity that goes on in the stands during a game. We did a lot of networking. Our business bought season tickets and we took many of our clients to the park.

Can you imagine how ill with depression I would have to be if I couldn't even bring myself to go to a baseball game? Sometimes at games, I now look around and ponder how many people in the park are suffering from depression or contemplating suicide. For a period of time, I wasn't a mental health statistic in the crowd, I was one of the absentee statistics, the missing person whose seat was empty.

If you feel that you have disconnected from life or you are experiencing thoughts of self-harm, know that there is help. Contact https://talksuicide.ca or call 1-833-456-4566 toll free.

FIRST SIGN

In 1970, I graduated high school from Dakota Collegiate in Winnipeg, Manitoba. I went on to the University of Manitoba and convocated in 1975 with a Commerce degree in Business Math. Immediately, I started working at Great West Life in the Group Underwriting Department.

I became an insurance underwriter. That means I would analyze data and recommend whether to accept or reject an insurance application based on risk.

From the fall of 1975 to fall of 1976, things were going along quite well. I got along with my co-workers, I liked my work, and I even received a promotion. I had a vibrant social life outside work, dating and playing baseball. I seemed to be living a normal, new-to-the-working-world kind of life most young people in their early twenties experienced.

However, this so-called normal life did not continue in a normal direction. I started to feel a lot of anxiety. I felt helpless at times and did not always make good personal decisions. I don't know how the depression started and I wasn't aware of it happening, but I was going further and further in a dark direction.

I was always sensitive to people telling me what I should think or how I should feel. Heading into spring 1977, I walked away from relationships, friends, and life in general because I was taking on the weight of negative comments from too many negative people. For example, I was told by someone close to me that I was "too" obsessed with baseball. I shrugged my shoulders and walked away, but the comment didn't leave me. My love of baseball was, and continues to be, an integral part of who I am. I asked myself why someone would say that. Was my focus on baseball wrong? I didn't know, but I had already been pulled far enough down the negative spiral that I didn't even notice that I was drifting away from everyone and everything, even baseball.

By the summer of 1977, I was experiencing very severe depression, but I didn't know it. I didn't feel good, but I put it down to my negative interactions with others. (In 2002, many years later, my doctor had a different perspective. He wondered if the depression caused me to wallow in negative interactions.) Regardless of the why and how, by 1977, depression had solidly set in. I felt awful. At this time, I didn't even know that I was experiencing depression. Therefore, I didn't know how to get help or what to do. In this instance, I was the typical male who doesn't talk about what's going on inside. I expected that I would just figure it out on my own.

One day, my friend Doug and I were playing catch. We had

grown up together and both ended up becoming starting pitchers. He had recently graduated from university and was planning to go backpacking around Europe. He asked me if I wanted to go and I eagerly accepted. We planned to leave in October 1977.

Around the same time, I noticed my productivity at work was diminishing and this bothered me. I thought perhaps that taking the holiday would rejuvenate me and I would regain my enthusiasm for my work. Throughout the summer, I tried to get my productivity back up at work so I could leave work on high note. I was concerned that I was going to be fired because of declining job performance. My supervisor had commented that I was just not working the way I used to. There was an ebb and flow to my work. Sometimes I would be right back on my game and doing quite well. Other days, I was totally ineffective – like waves. (I later learned that this is a normal function of depression. As if *anything* about depression is normal.)

If I didn't even know what depression was, how could I possibly deal with the impact?

I struggled with work from spring until I left in October. My friends told me years later that I simply disappeared from their lives during those months. I would just work and go home. I never socialized. I stopped playing poker with my buddies. I didn't go to baseball games. Sometimes I would show up at family events, but I would be very quiet and withdrawn. I often wonder if times have changed enough that now somebody, anybody - family, friends, colleagues - would say something and maybe even stage an intervention. But in the 1970s, we didn't talk about things like mental health or emotions, especially men. It was dangerous and wrong then to discuss it. We now know it will always be dangerous and wrong to **not** talk about mental health.

In October, I was fully prepared to tender my resignation before I left for Europe. One of the last conversations that I had with my manager before I left had a lasting impact on me.

I was brutally honest with him. "I don't really know what's going on—but—I'm going to go travelling and maybe figure things out," I told him.

I knew something wasn't right but didn't know what it was or what I needed to do to make it better. My words were pensive and uncertain as I continued, "Could I please have a leave of absence?"

"John, you are a very productive employee and we're glad to have you here. Why don't you take all the time you need and come and see me when you get back?" Then he joked, "If you get to London, bring back Big Ben. I could use a new alarm clock."

Wow! *Take all the time you need.* To this day, I am still amazed at my manager's approach that was clearly in the best interest of his employee. Not only did I feel incredibly supported by my manager, he went further and negotiated an open leave of absence. This was significant as I would have a job when I returned and my health insurance stayed in place. Double wow!

I don't know why he did that for me. He didn't have to. At a time when mental health was never discussed, he seemed to know that I needed some guidance and support. From his perspective, I had potential, but it was more than that. I was just a young kid working in his first job. Why invest in someone who was showing signs of problems? To this day, I am deeply indebted to him because of the way he handled the situation.

Doug and I left in October 1977. I was overseas for three and a half months. I went to museums, met new people, visited different countries and stayed in hostels. While I travelled around Europe, although I didn't realize it at the time, I was self-treating for depression. I started writing and diarizing and delving into what makes my life good. In the bubble of backpackers and international camaraderie, life was good and I got better.

I've been told many times that depression starts to show up in our early twenties. I am a perfect example of that. I lived through my first bout of depression with the help of a very supportive manager and non-intentional, accidental self-treatment. Life moved on and I still didn't realize that I suffered from depression.

When I came home from Europe in early January 1978, I felt rejuvenated and ready to return to work. I went to Great West Life and stopped by my former manager's office. I walked in and declared, "I'm home and ready to go to work."

My manager looked at me. "There's a desk," he said, pointing in the direction of a vacant work station. "You're an underwriter. Start underwriting."

As easy as that, I was back to work, mentally healthy from my backpacking trip through Europe. My previous immediate supervisor was still at Great West Life but in a different area so I had a new supervisor. She was just as supportive. I was happy and once again a productive employee.

Outside of work, I did what normal young people do in their twenties: work, go out with friends, date, have fun. I was happy. I also spent a lot of time curling—after all, I live in Manitoba.

For the next twenty-four years, I did not have any symptoms of depression. I can't say that it was because I learned how to cope and prevent a recurrence. (I didn't know that I had experienced depression, so I wasn't consciously trying to prevent a recurrence.) I just went through a period where there were no significant triggers that would send me on the dark, downward spiral of depression.

This is apparently very common. You can have depression in your twenties and it might never affect you again. Or, it might reappear, even years later.

The family dynamics that often lay the seeds for depression in later years were not triggering me either. Our family members had quirks like any other family, but we were getting along reasonably well. Yet we also had things that were not talked about. There was a deep, dark family secret regarding my paternal grandfather, Stefan. He had suicided at age 57 (which was before I was born). No one talked about this. I could have been helped in my twenties if I had only understood my family dynamics and our unspoken history. It all came down to talking about what didn't matter and not talking about what did.

Sometimes suicide ideation is hereditary, sometimes it is not. Regardless, if you are experiencing thoughts of suicide, reach out. Contact https://talksuicide.ca or call 1-833-456-4566 toll free.

FAMILY AND ARCHETYPES

All families seem to deal with some kind of dysfunction. Mine had a lot. When I was growing up, we were never allowed to express frustration or anger in our house. It was something that we would just not do. If my mother saw us display a glimmer of anger, she quickly shut down our behaviour. As a child, I would be frustrated and confused. I would feel anger, but I was forbidden to express it. It was bottled up inside with no avenue for release. The anger just stayed inside me, which is a very dangerous place for it to reside.

Anger is a natural emotion and should be released in healthy ways. If it isn't, it can be corrosive and damaging. I have heard it said that "depression can be caused by anger turned inwards."

In our household, when we were asked to do something,

there would always be a plan that was expected to be executed as directed and my mother would expect my sisters and me to seamlessly adjust to any change that she made. I was not allowed to say," Aw geez, Mom." Any negative emotion was not acceptable. She would just command, "Don't be angry." Our only choice was to try to accommodate the changes which were demanded. If we questioned the changes, my mother would snap back, "Did you hear what I said?"

For example, on a particular Monday, my mom announced, "I want to have guests for supper next Sunday. I want all of you to clean the house on that morning. After supper, I want to show the guests our slides of our latest trip to Los Angeles. Johnny, you will show the slides."

Then on the Thursday, four days later, she said, "I have changed my mind. We will have our guests over on Saturday."

As a teenager, I had plans for Saturday that I didn't want to surrender. I said, "Mom, I have plans for Saturday. A group of my friends and I are going out to see a movie."

My mother said, "You can do that on Sunday."

I responded, "But Mom ..."

I started to protest. I was shut down by my mother's strong voice. "Did you hear what I said?" Case closed.

The anger created in me was due to my not being allowed to express this emotion and discharge it.

I loved my mother dearly and she did many good things. But like all of us, she was a flawed person and her negative behaviour had a detrimental impact on me as I grew up. She was a very social person and loved entertaining and having people over to celebrate birthdays, anniversaries and other special occasions. Each time, however, everything had to be perfect. The table was always perfectly set. The guest china was always perfectly placed with a name tag on each plate. We children were instructed to be the perfect helpers and always, always on our best behaviour. We were like actors on a stage.

When I watch the British sit-com "Keeping Up Appearances," I think of my mother who displayed many of the characteristics of the show's main character, Hyacinth Bucket. Not only was Hyacinth obsessed with keeping up appearances and maintaining an impeccable house, she was also always directing people's lives. My mother also wanted to keep up appearances and control others, traits that create considerable mental stress. Hyacinth and my mother would put on a front. (My mother's twin brother was the exact opposite. My Uncle Fred didn't care about keeping up appearances. We pointed this out to my mother many times. She just wouldn't listen.) She wanted the family on display, like in a fishbowl. We were like props or actors on a stage to make her look good.

When relatives visited Winnipeg, my mother would inevitably want to host a huge party. We were used to all the entertaining but would always be worn out by the time everyone eventually left. At some point, my sisters and I said there were too many parties. We didn't get a chance to visit one on one with anyone. My mother would organize our relatives' timetables. These family members would in turn tell us that they didn't like it. We would communicate this to our mother, but our words were like an annoying fly buzzing near her ear, an annoyance that would eventually be waved away.

Unfortunately, some of our relatives began to avoid visiting us in Winnipeg in order to elude the mandatory parties that my mother would hold. She drove away the very people she wanted to be close to. I feel sad looking back that no one felt empowered to force her to hear and adjust to what we were saying. Not only for our sakes but hers as well—I can't imagine the energy required to plan and be the "perfect host."

I first became interested in *archetypes* during my stay in hospital after my suicide attempt. Archetypes are a way to describe personality traits. They also help explain why interactions between people can create conflict. Delving into archetypes helped me considerably as I began to examine my parents, myself, and our interactions. I studied the ideas of author Caroline Myss in order to understand how the personality traits of my family members affected me. I had to learn that my parents are flawed human beings just like me and not to blame my mother and father for my depression—but understanding archetypes helped me to understand how certain traits had such a profound negative effect on me. My learning was about awareness and how to safely interact with those archetypes.

I learned that my mother had a Queen archetype, which means she craved control and needed to consistently get her way. She could make many people cave into her demands. She conditioned her children to never challenge her. This "dark side" of a Queen archetype got her what she wanted, but it alienated many people and drove them away from her. There is an expression, "Your parents know how to push your buttons because they installed those buttons." So ever since we were kids, we were conditioned to do what my mother wanted. If she didn't get her way, she would get angry, pout or try to make us feel guilty—so we would cave.

Archetypes have both positive aspects and a dark, shadowy side. They describe people's personality traits and provide a foundation for what we think and what we believe, in other words, what drives us to do what we do.

The most impactful archetype to me while I was growing up was the Queen archetype. The Queen runs the show. Demonstrating the actions of the Queen archetype, my mother was a take-charge type of person. She was very social and was the Queen of entertaining, pun intended. She would assign who would do what and we were expected to listen and follow. A Queen can act with benevolence and kindness. I give my mother full credit for having a kind heart. She always meant well. But the shadow side of her Queen archetype would bring out her need for absolute control to maintain order and perfect appearances. I had no idea how to cope with her shadow side until I educated myself on the power of archetypes.

When I started exploring archetypes, it was important to my learning to understand archetypes as neither good nor bad. I searched for comic examples of Queens to balance the intensity of the negativity side of the Queen archetype. I found it okay to laugh at the most comical form that I could find of a Queen archetype - *Alice in Wonderland's* Queen of Hearts when she doesn't get her way and she yells, "Off with their heads!" The comic relief helped me to keep perspective as I looked at my family members with a new understanding.

My mother was a twin. From my conversations with people who were twins or who know twins, I have come to believe that it is common for them to crave attention because they often wouldn't get enough attention when they were young. I think that my mother fit the pattern because she did have to find ways to attract attention away from her twin brother. I would say that my mother was self-centred but usually not in a mean-spirited way. She did a lot of good things but she craved attention. It was often all about her. For example, my younger sister's birthday is on October 24th. My mother's birthday was on October 28th. My birthday is on November 3rd. Instead of having a birthday celebration for each of us, my mother would orchestrate a celebration on her birthdate (October 28th). We only celebrated one day, but it was always the date of her birth, not mine or my sister's.

My mother's sister Ida was one of the few who could reject my mother's control. One day during a shopping trip to the Hudson's Bay store with my mother, Aunt Ida found a piece of memorabilia that she knew I would like. She told my mother, "I'm going to get this for John."

My mother didn't like what Aunt Ida was about to do. "I don't want to watch you spend that amount of money." She knew Aunt Ida didn't have much money, as she was a single parent raising three sons.

Aunt Ida simply said, "Then don't watch me." That was a powerful moment. Aunt Ida had inadvertently given us children an example and the courage to see that we could stand up to a

Queen archetype who is out of control.

My sisters and I had a hard time handling our mother's drive for control. We all tried to find our own way to counter her behaviour and its effect on each of us. It was easier for me when I lived in Saskatoon, Saskatchewan from 1981 to 1986. I was finally free to do anything that I wanted. My mother and father came to visit me only once. Most of the time I went home to Winnipeg to visit. I gave no advance notice that I was coming. I would contact my parents once I arrived in the city so my mother wouldn't be able to plan the large parties that were so important to her.

Many years passed. I was an adult myself before I was able to identify and understand my mother's drive for the need for control and the appearance of perfect order in her family. Did she know herself what drove her behaviour? Was it fear? Insecurity? Both? Or something completely different? I sometimes wonder how exhausting it must have been for her to never let go of that control.

In 1982, I met a wonderful woman in Saskatoon. Jan. She was, and will always be, the love of my life. When I took Jan to Winnipeg the first time, I didn't tell my parents that I was coming to the city. We flew down on Friday to attend an office function. I called my parents on Saturday to tell them that I was in town and that Jan was with me. I suggested that we meet on Sunday. We got together for lunch at a restaurant. The rest of the afternoon was filled up with visiting at my parents' home. Just the immediate family were there, as my mother did not have enough time to arrange a larger function. We had a nice afternoon and supper and returned to Saskatoon. It was one of the easiest adult visits I had had with my parents. This was no doubt due to the fact that I only informed my mother that I was in the city when I was shortly about to leave it. I had limited the amount of time that could be controlled by my mother to a mere afternoon.

In 1987, Jan came with me when I moved back to Winnipeg. I told her that we didn't want to find a place too close to my parents. Jan asked why and I just said, "Trust me." We lived far enough away that my mother couldn't just drop in. Over the years, Jan and I tried to host a few family gatherings, but my mother, the Queen archetype, would inevitably take over and run the gatherings. So, we just stopped having family gatherings at our house.

Regardless of my mother's attempts at control and my inability to cope with it, she was kind underneath. A King or Queen archetype can do good things. But if the shadow side gets out of control, then those archetypes can cause considerable destruction.

My mother, always in control, would not hear of anything beyond what she could control. She had to always portray the happy wife and mother who was known for her entertaining. She needed to keep up the appearance of the self-assured woman with a normal family. My depression would definitely not fit in with what she perceived our family should be. After my suicide attempt on September 19th, 2002, I spent six weeks in the mental health ward in the Victoria Hospital. My dear father visited me every day. My mother only came to visit me once, dressed as if she was going out to a party. She never accepted that anything she had done had remotely contributed to my problems.

My father opened up and we worked together in the healing process. He came to understand that his actions of physical discipline, such as when he cuffed me about my ears or gave me a kick in the behind, had been damaging to me. It was humiliating when he did this in front of others, especially in public. Times throughout my childhood when he went three or four days without speaking a word to me were also part of his damaging actions, even though they weren't physical. The silent treatment itself can be hurtful.

From early ages, my sisters and I were conditioned to not express anger or frustration. During my childhood and teenage years, I was abnormally moody from time to time. If I felt down, I would simply withdraw and I would drop out of sight. My moodiness continued into my adult years. What is normal moodiness? Something that would last an hour or two or maybe a day? Many of my friends would notice my moodiness because it would last a few days or maybe a week.

I believe that my suppressed anger caused me to be moody. It wasn't just about being angry if I didn't get my own way. In life we can't always get our own way. When a plan didn't go as it was supposed to, I wasn't allowed to vent. I was not allowed to be angry. I can see now that I was never taught the skills to manage disappointment. Learning to deal with disappointment helps to teach resiliency. I lost out on that opportunity to learn about resiliency during my childhood and teenage years.

Not only did my supressed anger lead to a lack of resiliency—I believe it led to depression.

I am very close with three of my sisters: Pauline, Susan, and Beverley. I'm in the middle, born after Susan. At age 23, I dealt with depression and I didn't even know it. Prior to my suicide attack at age 50, my siblings had very little knowledge of my bouts with depression but my friends knew. Isn't that often the case? Our families are the last to know.

Like the Queen archetype, the King archetype craves attention and absolute control at all times over those in his kingdom. If they do not have this control, they will obtain it in any way they can, not caring nor even realizing how this grab for control may be alienating and damaging others.

My father had a King archetype and possessed a domineering presence and powerful voice. He insisted on making the final decision, even ending all contradicting discussion. Even once we were all adults, he continued to try to trump all our decisions. For example, if we were driving in a vehicle, my father insisted on the route we must take, even if he wasn't behind the wheel. He continued to do this to his dying days.

From what I have learned from family, I believe my paternal grandfather had a King archetype. Of the many King traits that he would have exhibited, I'm guessing based on his business accomplishments that he had a clear vision and purpose. He exhibited traits like a high opinion of himself, holding power through demanding obedience, and not tolerating disagreement.

Grandfather operated both at home and in the business world through intimidation, a strategy not uncommon in many business people. He was a very hard-working and industrious man. The City of Winnipeg hired him to remove snow from the city streets. His oldest son, Pete drove a truck for his father's business. One time, Pete picked up a load of snow then drove to the riverbank to dump the snow. He backed up the truck but when he raised the box for the snow to fall out, the tailgate fell off and rolled down to the frozen river. Pete hurried down to get the tailgate and fell through the ice. He didn't go home to dry off and change his clothes. He was too terrified about losing time and incurring his father's wrath. So wet and cold, he kept working. He got sick with pneumonia and died shortly after. My grandfather's extreme King archetype cost him his oldest son.

I believe that my father also possessed some of those King traits of intimidation and wrath. My father's generation, and even my generation, grew up thinking that a father's word was final and disagreeing or disappointing your father would bring considerable negative consequences. My father treated me like he had been taught through his father's example.

My grandfather was an alcoholic. According to stories from his daughter, bootleggers would come to their house. My grandfather would take samples of the whiskey that they were selling. He would light the sample. If it didn't burn with the appropriate colour, he wouldn't buy it. My father consumed alcohol in large quantities. Again, like father like son.

My father grew up the second youngest of nine children. His mother died when he was five years old. According to my uncles, there was not a lot of love and affection in that household. My mother grew up in a much more loving household. My father often talked about the first time he went to my mother's house where he saw what a normal family dinner was like. They treated each other with respect. This was because my mother's mother, Amy, was kind and gentle with an open mind. She taught her children and later her grandchildren that all religions basically boiled down to one thing: be good to one another and respect all people. My father learned to behave with more kindness due to her influence, but he was still prone to fits of anger.

When my father became angry, the episode would last for three to four days. During those angry times, we would walk around the house on eggshells. We were not allowed to get angry—only my father was permitted to show his anger.

Despite their archetype shadow flaws, my parents did good things for us. If we took a ledger and made two columns of good things on one side and bad things on another, there would be many examples in both columns. Understanding how my parents' behaviour impacted me is simply a recognition. It is not a blame game.

In life, there are times when we just can't walk away from people with unhealthy archetypes. However, if we have to be in some kind of relationship with these types of people, we can choose to reduce exposure or set more boundaries.

When I look back at how my family dynamics and family history contributed to drawing me in the downward spiral toward the suicide attack in the river, I am amazed at the normal years where I was happy with my work and my social life. In 1987, when I was 35, Jan and I married. I appreciate what she brings to my life. She has been at my side through everything. I am grateful for the good years we had before the return of the ebb and flow of depression. I am grateful for the years we had as I recovered from depression. And now, twenty years since my attempt to suicide, I am even more grateful for her love.

Suicide eliminates all other options. If you are experiencing thoughts of suicide, please seek help. Contact https://talksuicide.ca or call 1-833-456-4566 toll free.

RISE ABOVE

DOWNWARD TRAJECTORY

I believe that there were two factors at play which put me on a downward trajectory. The first was my predisposition to depression and the second was my business relationship.

Starting in the 1990s, there were a number of significant changes in my life. On the personal side, Jan and I moved into a house that would become our home for over two decades.

On the professional side, I had gone out on my own and became an independent life insurance and investment advisor. I went into business with another independent agent who was about 20 years older than me. My partner was gruff, but a good businessman and for the first seven years or so, we made good money.

However, during our first year in business together, his wife had a stroke and her health deteriorated painfully and slowly until she died in 1997.

My partner changed when his wife died. Much too late, I found out that he had serious issues of his own which he hid from me and those we worked with. He was a great salesman. He covered his flaws well, so it took me quite a while to see how his bad personal and business decisions were taking him down and affecting those around him.

A confluence of factors sent me once again into depression. In the summer of 2002, I only went to two ball games. That was it. I gave the tickets away for the rest of the year. I don't remember how I felt about not being at the ball park. I was overwhelmed with the depression itself. The fact that I watched a lot of baseball as I began to recover (first in the hospital and then later when I returned home) tells me how important the game is to me and how significant it was that I had no desire to be at the ball park during 2002 when the depression had its grip on me.

I've spent a lot of time since my suicide attack pondering how I feel when baseball is pushed out of my life - how I feel when it's not there. If I get into a situation today where I become disinterested in baseball, I will go talk to a psychologist because this disinterest is a sure sign that something huge is going on with my mental health.

The relationship with my business partner continued to deteriorate. We fought all the time. We experienced financial stress but the business was still in the black until early 2002. A few times, I offered to buy him out but my offers were always declined. Interest rates were coming down which only added to my workload as we needed to sell higher volumes to realize the same level of net income. I began to see my partnership as an increasing liability for me. One of my friends later commented that, "John, you have an anvil around your neck."

What I experienced is very common for those who suffer from depression. We take on more and more stress while depression infuses us like a steady drip that eventually becomes a flow of pain. During the spring of 2002, I finally booked an appointment with my family doctor because I wasn't sleeping well at all. He gave me a prescription for sleep. After about a week, I still wasn't sleeping. I went back and told him that I needed something stronger. He said that what he gave me should have knocked me out.

Then he said four words: "John, you have depression."

It's quite a concept to try to absorb for the first time. I thought, *Wow.*

I really didn't know much about depression. So, to hear that word describing what was wrong with me was startling. But he wasn't done.

"You've had this before."

How did he know that?

"Why would you say that?" I asked. His statement seemed out of the blue.

"It's very rare at age 50 to experience depression for the first time. I'm sure that you've experienced depression in the past."

I was still absorbing that I have depression, but my doctor was probing more.

"Do you have a history of depression in your family? Is it in your family tree?"

My doctor's comments and questions were both shocking and revealing.

"Yes, several aunts and uncles on both sides have had depression—and my grandfather suicided."

"John, it's not an automatic to have depression if there is a family history of depression. However, you would be predisposed because depression is in your family."

He booked an appointment for me to see a psychiatrist. I was hopeful that I could get rid of my depression. During the drive home from my doctor's office, I was terribly confused. It took me a long time, months and years, to put my diagnosis of depression into perspective.

Jan was already at home. I asked her to sit down as I had something to tell her. We sat on the couch and I took her hand as we sat side by side. Tears began to roll down my cheeks.

"My doctor said that I have depression."

Jan seemed to be as shocked as I was at this diagnosis.

I had gradually withdrawn from a lot of things. We wouldn't go out much. I had stopped going to the monthly poker games with my friends. Even my solace, my piece of heaven, the ball park – I had only gone a couple of times in all in 2002. So, something was definitely not right.

It must be hard for people to watch loved ones go through pain. I can't imagine what it has been like for Jan to watch me go through depression and feel helpless to change the situation. She has never left my side. She is the love of my life and has been with me every step of the way of my recovery journey.

"My doctor is going to refer me to a psychiatrist," I told Jan. It was the first time that we had looked at what was wrong with me in terms of depression.

The next day, the psychiatrist's office called me for an appointment. Yes. One day later.

After I told Jan, she asked, "What is it telling you that within a day your doctor got you in to see the psychiatrist?"

"It's good that it's happening," I responded. I became hopeful that the psychiatrist would be able to help me.

"I think that your doctor is very worried about you," Jan said.

For the past three weeks, I had not slept for more than one or two hours per night. When I met with the psychiatrist, he prescribed a sleep-inducing medication.

Roles may vary in other provinces or in different countries, but in Manitoba a psychiatrist is a medical doctor who specializes in mental health. Psychiatrists understand the link between mental and physical problems. They diagnose and treat mental, emotional and behavioural disorders. They manage treatment and provide therapy for very serious mental illnesses. They also prescribe medication.

When it comes to medication, treating depression is not like treating a cold where you take a pill to stop your nose from dripping or cough syrup to soothe a cough. It takes a while to find the right drug and the proper dosage. I had no idea how long it would take to find the right medication solution.

In a follow-up visit, my family doctor said that there are two routes out of depression. One is medication and the other is talk therapy. My family doctor saw talk therapy, sometimes referred to as psychotherapy, as a good route for me to explore. That was the first time I had heard of talk therapy. But I had never thought about medication for mental health either and now I was both seeing a psychiatrist and preparing to visit a psychologist.

After I first heard the term "talk therapy", I learned more about the role of the psychologist. Like psychiatrists, they understand how the brain works along with our feelings, emotions and thoughts. They must complete their first university degree in the field of psychology and have a master's degree in a related field. Many go on to obtain a PhD and become clinical psychologists specialized in the diagnosis and treatment of mental illness.

I was very disappointed that the medication prescribed by the psychiatrist was not the easy way out that I had hoped. It didn't help at all. I still wasn't sleeping.

In the meantime, I started calling psychologists. I met with a few of them. I felt good going to each appointment, hopeful that this might be the solution. But by the end of each appointment, my hope was dashed and I only experienced more disappointment. This was because we just didn't connect. I wasn't relating to any of the psychologists I met with. I didn't hear or sense anything in those appointments that I thought would really help me.

I started wondering—would the talk therapy only work once the medication kicked in?

I was very frustrated.

As the summer of 2002 wore on, my emotions were gradually disappearing, with the exception of increasing anxiety. My grandfather had suicided when my father was in his early twenties. During the summer, my twisted, depressed mind made me think many times that maybe my grandfather had the right idea. I was wrong to think that, but depression pulls us down a sorry path, blocking the right thoughts from getting in.

If anyone reading this is experiencing thoughts of suicide, know that there is help available. Reach out to your doctor or a suicide prevention line. Only recently has society recognized that suicide-ideation (thinking about suicide) is a real phenomenon. There are resources available for those experiencing it and many people are now reaching out for help. **Reaching out for help is a strength, not a weakness. A real sign of courage.**

My grandfather, Stefan emigrated from Ukraine. He arrived in Canada shortly after 1900. The Canadian government was recruiting people from Eastern Europe to come to Canada, specifically to come to the Prairies to break the land. Stefan met a Polish woman, Paulina, in Canada and they married. They homesteaded in Meleb, close by the town of Gimli, Manitoba.

My grandparents' first five children were born in Meleb. The family donated land to build a church, a school, and a railway siding. They moved to Saskatchewan for a year or two and then settled in Winnipeg on McFarlane Street in the Point Douglas area.

Stefan had horses. He was in the business of moving goods for short distances by dray horses. In 1925, he was one of the people contracted to excavate and clear the mud to make way for the Hudson's Bay building which is a major landmark in downtown Winnipeg. In the late 1920s, when he could see that horses were on the way out and trucks were coming in, he moved into the trucking business. He also had a construction business, building and selling houses.

In the late 1940s, my grandfather received a letter from the tax people informing him that he had never filed income tax and to please send his records. As my Aunt Ruth later told us, my grandfather pointed to his head, stating, "Records, what records? It's all up here." He dealt in cash so there were no cheques, invoices or statements.

The letter started to weigh on his mind and he was worried that he would be sent to prison. He was from Eastern Europe and that's how people were often treated there when they came into conflict with the government. He was scared that he would lose his holdings – trucks, houses, everything.

At 57, he hung himself in the basement of one of the houses that he had built.

At the time, my father would have been in his early twenties. He had served in the war and now that the war was over, he was training to be a fire fighter for the City of Winnipeg. On the day that my grandfather hung himself, my father was at No. 1 Station for training.

His brother Jake arrived at the station in a taxi. "The old man just died," he told his brother. "Come with me."

My mother told me that my father had wanted to talk to my grandfather about the letter from the tax people. He had more education than his older brothers and thought he could help. The older brothers were very much of the mindset from Eastern Europe where you don't talk to your parents about their business and convinced my father to just let my grandfather work it out on his own. I sometimes wonder if my father felt some responsibility that he didn't try hard enough to help. It is common after a suicide that friends and family question whether they could have done more, if they could have done something to prevent that final decision.

The family experienced a considerable amount of shame and stigma as a result of my grandfather's decision. The Catholic Church would not allow my grandfather to be buried in the Catholic cemetery where he had purchased a plot. That was the location where he had buried his first wife, Paulina, who died in 1930 and his son, Peter, who died shortly after.

No one ever talked about my grandfather's suicide. When

I was 17 years old, I was first made aware of how he died when my mother mentioned it accidentally. I learned more about what happened from my Aunt Gertrude who was married to Uncle Tom, one of my father's older brothers. Ironically, it was an in-law that told me the truth of the secret that was held so closely by my family members. Once my grandfather's death became more public within the family, we did talk about it - but never with my father.

When you get to a crisis point, like my grandfather was likely in, like I was in, your mind really starts to go in a bad direction. I was not looking logically at my grandfather's suicide. I was dangerously empathizing with him. I had no idea if it was a psychologically genetic or a learned behaviour.

That whole summer, the love of my life, Jan was trying to figure it out what she could do. She is a pharmacist and knows what medications can do to our mental and physical beings. She had never seen or experienced what I was going through. She felt helpless and powerless, not knowing what she could do to get me through whatever this was.

If you feel a loved one is near a crisis point in their life, do not wait for them to make a decision that can not be taken back. Contact https://talksuicide.ca or call 1-833-456-4566 toll free.

A PLAN BRINGS CALM

I was tired of trying medication that didn't seem to be working. I had already decided that a psychologist wouldn't be able to help me before the psychiatrist narrowed down the dose and type of medication, I didn't see a way out. I felt nothing but despair.

How do we feel when we make a significant decision? How does someone who is depressed feel when making a dangerous one? A decision where all options end? We feel desperate!

I found myself heading towards a difficult decision that would deliver what I wanted—or what I perceived that I needed. I didn't consider how my decision could impact Jan or my family and friends. When you are that deep in depression, you don't consider the people you will impact; you only want to end the pain you are experiencing.

Emotions affect decisions, good or bad. They also can affect the speed of arriving at a decision. My inability to identify any positive options certainly affected this life-altering—or rather, life-ending—decision. Was I impatient to get out, to find a way out, for something to change? Was I even capable of making a reasonable decision? My decision in late August was to get away from the pain by ending my life.

During the summer of 2002, the depression was driving my decisions and actions. From the outside, it would have been logical for someone to question whether I was even in charge of my own decisions. Right or wrong, rational or irrational, within my control or out of my control, I had my plan. Then it simply became how and when to execute.

I had maintained friendship with a group of high school friends. I was simply Big John to them because of my height. We had been getting together on a regular basis for years. At times, wives were included, sometimes they weren't. In January 2002, we started talking about how to commemorate our 50th birthdays. We settled on the weekend following the Labour Day weekend at Clear Lake, Manitoba where we would stay at one of the resort hotels with our wives – us four guys and three of our partners. When we discussed and booked our Clear Lake weekend, I had no idea where the next eight months would take me. I am still amazed at how much changed over the span of those eight months. I was troubled in January when we had our planning conversation, but at that time, I certainly did not have an understanding of how my downward spiral would pull me into the deep dark hole.

I decided to stay in this world until after the 50th birthday celebration. I wasn't going to leave before the event in September.

I didn't want anyone to have a bad time at the celebration. I wanted my friends to be happy and enjoy themselves. Then, I would carry out the plan only a few days after. Many people find it odd that someone who suicides has this calm, cheerful demeanor shortly before their death. But for me, it was simple. I had a plan that would end my pain. The decision was made. In a strange way, this relieved me of the pain.

I know now that depression is like an ebb and flow of water lapping on a shore. The depression is bad; then sometimes it seems to disappear. When my depression took me to the point of making a plan to end my life, it was no longer about an ebb and flow. Instead, it was like an eerie calm before the storm. I was calm, relaxed and ready to enjoy the weekend. You see, making the decision and having a plan released me from my burden of pain. Someone asked me once to describe how bad the pain was. All I can say is that it is the worst pain I have ever experienced. Unless you have been there, you could never understand it.

Jan and I packed up and drove to Clear Lake, about a three-hour drive from Winnipeg. We arrived on the Friday and checked in at the Cedar Resort. The weather matched my calmness. It's beautiful to be in Riding Mountain National Park in late summer and early fall. Leaves are starting to turn colours. During the day, the late summer sun warmed us enough that we didn't need to wear jackets and the evenings cooled down so we slept well in the fresh air away from the city.

Our Friday supper set the tone for the seven of us. We ate good food. We laughed and reminisced about high school, amazed that we graduated thirty-two years earlier. We finished supper and agreed to call it a night. After all, we were 50 years young and we wanted to be in fine form for our golf game the next day.

The next day while our wives explored the resort and gift shops, we golfed. We were like teenagers back in high school, living it up on the golf course.

It was very windy. One of my friends commented, "This wind is killing my drives."

"Then I guess that you will believe me that I had to blow the same fart three times," I quipped back at him.

I was known for comments like that and for also being John, "the Jokester." I was in a great mood on the golf course, keeping up a steady flow of one-liners.

Sunday arrived too quickly. We had breakfast together, packed up and left. During the drive home, Jan and I slipped into our normal road-trip conversation. We talked about our dogs, Monty, Chapin, Fancy and Piper. When we were away, they were always top in our minds. We knew how glad they would be to see us.

During that September long weekend at Clear Lake, I was happy, almost euphoric. Unknown to anyone else, I was happy *because* I had made the decision to end my pain by ending my life. Even years later when I speak of my decision and what it was like for me for the weeks that followed, I can still feel the happiness and calm that I experienced throughout the Clear Lake weekend. I knew what no one else knew—my pain was going to be over soon.

Please know that people experiencing depression and suicidal thoughts don't necessarily know how to reach out for help. This is why it is so important for all of us to talk openly without judgment, reprisal or ridicule about what we are thinking and feeling. I wish everyone could open up about negative thoughts about how we value ourselves and perceive our self-worth.

My decision to end my pain put me in a very good mood. One of my friends who was at Clear Lake told me later that he was happy to see me so happy because he knew that I was wrestling with depression.

Once while visiting me in hospital, he asked me an important question, "Big John, how could you be so happy at our 50th birthday weekend then a few days later swim into the river?"

My friend was deeply bothered about the contrast between what I had projected that weekend and what was actually going on inside my mind. He had a terrible time believing that only a few days after a happy, fun weekend, I could swim into the river intent on ending my life.

I tried to explain that my *decision* to end my pain by suicide had, in effect, ended my emotional pain. It was only because I had made this decision that I was able to enjoy the weekend to the extent that I did. This contradiction was a tough concept for him to grasp.

Watch for sudden happiness and/or calmness when someone is going through depression. This person may have a plan for self-harm. Don't hesitate to ask someone if they

feel suicidal. Do not hesitate to reach out to professionals or a mental health organization for the best way to support your friend or family member.

RIVER ATTACK!

When I woke up on Thursday morning, September 19, 2002, I was convinced that it was *The Day*. I got up and dressed in normal business attire, which for me was a dark blue blazer, pressed trousers, a white shirt and striped tie.

Once my wife left the house for her errands, I was alone. I took my medication and then recorded a final goodbye to Jan on my Dictaphone machine. I wanted to tell her how much pain I was in so she would understand why I had taken this step. The last thing that I remember saying to Jan in the recording was, "Have fun with the dogs." I took the tape with me and put it in the car and left the house for what I thought would be the last time.

I drove to a location by the Red River close to a launching spot for boats. Very few people go there in September. The summer green leaves were turning golden. A faint breeze rustled in aging leaves as the odd one flickered to the ground. I was sitting in my car and I remember being relieved that nobody else was there. I considered driving into the river via the boat launch.

I asked myself, "Should I do this? Should I not do this? Should I do this? Should I not do this?" Over and over, I asked the same contrasting questions. Where was a daisy with petals to pluck when you needed one?

While I sat there, every few minutes, I would pop a Clonazepam. It's an anti-anxiety medication like the more commonly known Valium.

I drove to another spot, about 100 yards behind a walking path and under a bridge. It was close to the Perimeter Highway and south of the University of Manitoba. It was there that I parked my vehicle.

I opened the door and got out of my car. I walked the short distance to the edge of the river.

I noticed cars going back and forth over the bridge 50-80 yards south of where I stood.

I thought, "I kind of hope that someone sees me. Maybe they will stop me."

It was a beautiful, warm, sunny day. I remember as I started to enter the river, the ground was muddy and soft under my shoes. I was surprised how warm the water was for mid-September. The riverbed dropped off very quickly. After only a few steps, I was in over my head and had to start swimming.

The Red River is known as a river with strong currents and it was flowing fairly fast as I swam. I could feel the current carrying me downstream but I didn't feel anything pulling me under. My dark blue blazer was saturated and heavy.

Suddenly, I was in the middle of the river. At that moment, I experienced something spiritual. My godmother Aunt Ida came to be with me. She had died a few years earlier. I could hear her voice.

"John, this is going to get better. Turn around and swim out. This is why I taught you to swim when you were eight years old." Aunt Ida was my mother's sister. When I was a kid, I used to go and spend summers at her place on Eagle Lake in northern Ontario. It was there that she taught me how to swim.

Then I heard my Uncle Tom's voice, joining hers. My father's brother was also deceased. He and I were more like brothers than uncle and nephew. Uncle Tom was a great friend to me as well as a great golfing partner.

"John, the golf courses here are great but it's not time for you to be here with me. You have work to do." By now, I had been carried 100 yards downstream "Go," he continued. "Swim out of the river. Get back to shore."

A sibling of each of my parents had told me to get out. Why them? Why someone on each side of the family? They both had experienced the multi generation cycle of mental challenges and had suffered in silence. Was this their way of telling me to break the cycle?

I was very close to Aunt Ida and Uncle Tom and something made me listen to their urging.

Someone asked me years later whether there was a moment of clarity or did I just swim out. That question really made me think about why I swam out. I swam into the river with zero hope for change. In my mental fog and darkness, Aunt Ida gave me hope. Uncle Tom gave me purpose. Somehow, somewhere a glimmer of optimism and courage broke through.

At that moment, I began to believe that things would improve. I changed my mind and shifted my intention. My internal voice said with determination, "John, get out of the river."

As I swam out, I hoped the current would not pull me down. I struggled in my sodden clothes. Aunt Ida's swimming lessons so many years ago helped me stay afloat. I could feel her teaching influence—which was ironic as she never learned to swim herself.

I remember being happy when I finally felt the muddy riverbed beneath my feet. It was a challenge moving forward in the mud. Eventually I broke free from the river and began to make my walk back to my car.

Children often like to feel the squish, squish of wet sand or mud squirming around their toes as they walk along a shore. I reminisced about pleasant barefoot squishes as I stumbled and crawled upstream to get to my car, my shoes smacking and glopping in and out of the mud. Somehow, with the same forces that got me out of the river, I slapped my muddy hands on the front hood and willed myself to fully stand.

My muddied hands opened the driver's door. I had left the keys in the ignition. I got in and started the car. I gripped the steering wheel tightly, leaving mud marks on it, evidence of my crawl through the *Red River gumbo*.

I don't remember much after that, but somehow I drove home. The next thing that I knew was standing in the driveway. I don't remember being wet or cold.

While I stood there, Jan arrived home from her errands and gave me a quizzical look. I was dripping in mud and water from head to toe.

She rolled down her car window and asked, "What happened? Did you get splashed by a car driving by?"

"I swam into the river," I replied

"We're going to the hospital," she said, jumping out of her car.

Some weeks later, Jan told me that she took me into the house, put me into the shower, and dressed me in dry clothes. I don't remember any of that. I have no idea how Jan held herself together as she cleaned me up and then drove me to the hospital.

I don't remember anything about the drive. I was still muddled up because of the anxiety and the overdose of Clonazepam.

The next thing I remembered was waking up in the psychiatric ward, pleading with one of the nurses to find the tape. I didn't want Jan to discover it and listen to what I had thought would be my last words. It was found and I destroyed it.

THOUGHTS FROM JAN

It was one day in 2001, as we got up in the morning, John said to me, "I think you better take me to the hospital. I can't breathe."

I thought he was having a heart attack. Without thinking, we got into the car and I drove him to Emergency. He was admitted to the Intensive Care Unit for an irregular heartbeat where he stayed for five days. At that point, we thought it was some kind of heart problem, probably caused by stress. From tests during those five days, we discovered that he had atrial fibrillation which is an irregular and often rapid heart rate that occurs when the two upper chambers of the heart experience chaotic electrical signals. The result is a fast and irregular heart rhythm.

John took several weeks off work. During this time, he would sleep during the day but not sleep at night. That went on for months. After a while, John went back to work but I knew something was still not right. I will never forget the day that John came home from his appointment with his general practitioner in the spring of 2002.

"My doctor told me that I have depression," he said.

I was stunned. I don't remember what I said to him. I was really worried. Probably, I asked him what medication the doctor had given him. As a pharmacist, it would make sense that I would ask him that. The doctor had prescribed anti-depressant and anti-anxiety medications.

Once John told me about the depression diagnosis, my mind went back over the events of the last two years - now in light of the diagnosis. Right away, I started second guessing myself. "Why didn't I see that?" I thought to myself.

I told John that he had to take the medication and that it would take a few months for everything to work. As the weeks passed, I noticed that he wasn't feeling any better. Actually, the medications made him feel worse. He was on such strong dosages during that period, he would alternately sleep several hours during the day, but little at night.

Heading into that summer, I was growing more concerned. I thought that there should have been an improvement. But we still didn't see progress. John was trying to go back to work. He was grumpy and none of the medications or treatments seemed to be working. We struggled to get the help we needed to get John the right medications and appropriate counseling—only to both feel discouraged. Things were not looking great.

I started to wonder how we were going to manage. How would we pay our bills if John could not work? We used his employee family assistance program to get counseling. If John could not go back to work, then I would have to start looking for a job. I knew I would not be able to earn as much as he had been earning. Would we have to sell our home and look for a smaller place?

I started to feel very overwhelmed and depressed. I needed to get help for myself.

At some point during the summer of 2002, I had gone to a Sheltie Dog club meeting. I came home and as I walked in from the garage to the laundry room, I registered a funny smell. I asked John about it, but he didn't really have an answer. He had some casual explanation, but I didn't pursue it further. As I look back now, I wish that I would have asked him more about it. Don't we always second guess ourselves when we look back and see the signs? I just accepted what he said. In retrospect, now as I connect the dots, I know it was the smell of car exhaust.

Later in his recovery, he told me that he did actually get into the car with the garage door closed with the intention of suiciding—but something stopped him.

Heading into the Clear Lake long weekend, the road trip down was very enjoyable. We had fun and enjoyed the scenery. It was just good to get away. I thought that John was pretty much his old self. It was because he was going to be with his friends, this group of high school fellows celebrating their 50th birthday year together.

On the morning of the day of the River Attack, John got ready for work. I headed out to run errands. When I got home, there was John, soaking wet standing in the driveway. I rolled down the window and said, "What happened? Did you get splashed by a car driving by?" I thought it was something harmless. It didn't immediately register that the real reason could have been something much darker.

John responded, "I swam into the river."

I switched to automatic pilot. I took him inside and took off all of his wet clothes, leaving them in a pile in the garage. Then I took him upstairs and put him in the shower. I was going on instinct. I cleaned him up, got him dressed and drove to the hospital. I walked up to the triage desk and told him that he went into the river. I was not in a mood for any fooling around and was very assertive—which is very unusual for me. They took us right in. The psychiatrist on call came fairly quickly.

He said, "I have to admit him right away."

I was so grateful that there was an available bed in the psychiatric ward because that is not always the case. While we were waiting in Emergency, I called John's sister, Susan and her daughter, Lisa. Once John was taken up to the ward, he was put into what they call a holding room. Any new admission has to stay there for the first 72 hours. Initially, we were allowed in, but then we had to say good bye. I was not going to be allowed to see John during those first 72 hours.

I drove home. It was weird to walk in the house by myself but at the same time I experienced a huge relief because I didn't have to worry about John.

After the 72 hours passed, it didn't take long for me to finally allow myself to have hope. John told me right away that he was going to do everything that the mental health experts asked him to do. He was assigned a nurse and she talked to John every evening. I remember thinking that this time, he may get the help he needed.

John's car was a mess but I didn't have the energy to do anything about it. Each time, I would drive away and come back, the dirty car with its telltale muddy hand marks would still be there unchanged.

After a few days, some friends called me and asked if there was anything that they could do for me. Usually, the thing I do is to deny help. But instead, I said, "You know what. I go out and come back every day and look at the muddy clothes and the muddy car. It really bothers me."

My friend Lesley and her husband Clyde came over right away. Lesley took John's muddy clothes to the dry cleaners and Clyde took the car through a car wash.

Problem solved; as Lesley would say: "Easy peasey."

When there is a mental health crisis, friends often don't know what to do or what to say. You don't need to know the answers, all you need to do is call and ask, "How can I help?"

RISE ABOVE

HANDPRINTS –
LISA'S STORY

I don't remember much of what happened before the phone call. If you asked me what I had seen or had eaten that day, or where I had been, I couldn't tell you. I know the phone rang just before 4:00 p.m. on September 19, 2002. I remember the tone in my Aunt Jan's voice as she said, "You need to come to Victoria Hospital. Is your mom home? It's your Uncle John."

"What's wrong?"

"Just come."

I remember running upstairs and telling my mother where we needed to be. We didn't have any details—only that something had happened to my Uncle Johnny.

Allow me to elaborate on my relationship with my uncle for a moment. My father struggled with an addiction to alcohol and as a result, our relationship was difficult and we had become estranged. My Uncle John had lovingly stepped into the father figure role for me. He was always there when I needed him. He helped provide me with opportunities that I might never have experienced. He helped to open doors that otherwise might have remained closed.

He ran a successful business. He was well-liked and a pillar in the community. He was involved in everything from sports to the arts. If you needed something, chances were my Uncle John knew someone who could help you with it. He was the safe place to fall when I was hurt and the voice that knew how to pick me back up so I could continue on. He always seemed unbreakable to me. He was my rock.

But on September 19, 2002, that rock tried to sink. I can't remember much about the drive to the hospital. It was a very quiet ride. I remember walking into the building. All the hallways looked the same. I could not get to him fast enough. Then, all of a sudden, there he was. And there we were. And the story began to unravel itself. My aunt told us what he had done or what he had tried to do.

My uncle tried to commit suicide by swimming fully clothed into the Red River.

I felt completely dazed. I was devastated that something had been hurting him so badly that he felt the only way out was to take himself out of this world. On the other hand, I was overjoyed that he was still lying in his hospital bed and I could hug him, kiss him, and tell him I loved him. It was not too late for that.

I remember the pain in my aunt's face and the break in her voice as she told us the rest of the story—how he had changed his mind and swam back, got back into his car and drove home. She had found him wearing his business suit. Dripping wet. I still don't know how she held herself together. I guess there is something to be said about true love—loving someone so much that your survival instincts kick in and your individual self becomes much less of a focus because the one you love is in pain.

I had to work at the ballpark that night. My uncle helped me get my job there. I told him I did not want to go. But he loves baseball so much and loves me so much, that he encouraged me to go. He didn't want me to miss the game. I did go to work that night and for the first time, I felt that I really began to understand why my uncle loves that game so much. There is something so therapeutic in the sound of the ball hitting the glove; in the way the red dust rises as a runner slides home; in the sound of the ball hitting that sweet spot on a wooden bat. I felt closer to my Uncle John that night than I ever had.

The secret was finally out—and that meant his depression would lose some of its power. Now he could finally find his path to healing.

It is an unsettling feeling to hear that your uncle cannot have his own clothes in the hospital because he is a risk to himself. But he handled everything with such dignity. He was so kind and courteous to everyone. He was willing to be helped and guided. It was as if he had allowed himself to be a lump of clay, permitting the doctors to help him get his shape back. He let the professionals do what they needed to do so that he could be on a path to recovery.

But I was scared that I would say or do the wrong thing. I was also scared that it would not work. I didn't understand what it meant to have depression. I was worried he could not be "fixed," as if he was "broken." But over the next few weeks, I learned that this was not the case.

You see, the stigma surrounding depression causes people to have difficulty communicating to their families that they are in depression. They worry, "What will they think of me? Will they think I am weak? Will they think I am being overdramatic? Will they think I'm crazy? Will they think I am broken?" My uncle was not any of those things. He most certainly was not broken. He did not need to be repaired. He had a challenge to overcome. What he needed was a professional to help guide him and provide him with tools to manage it rather than feeling as though the challenge was taking over his life.

We all have challenges in our lives. Sometimes we have things that happen in our bodies (such as chemical imbalances) that affect us to the point where we need to take medication to help create a balance. Sometimes we just need someone to talk to, to help us learn how to appropriately process and react to things that we feel. There are times when we need both. One of the most important things I learned from my uncle is that there is no shame in asking for help.

Every time someone feels a need to be silent about depression, life is at risk of being lost. The world cannot afford these tragedies. I visited my uncle in the hospital over the six weeks he was there. I am sure he will tell you the road has not been easy since he came home. He has been on a personal journey that has changed the way he sees the world, and to be completely honest, it has changed the way I see him. He is not the same uncle I knew when I was a little girl. I accept that some things about his personality have changed because he has had to change.

Recovery is also not easy for family members because we have to accept that sometimes behavioural changes need to be made in order for the individual suffering from depression to remain healthy. My uncle John is still a rock for me. That has never changed.

I remember going to my aunt and uncle's home in the weeks after his suicide attempt. My aunt opened the garage door and my uncle's car was parked inside. On the hood of his shiny, black Pontiac were two muddy handprints. They were clear as day and they streaked down the hood of the car, starting up by the windshield and then down towards the headlights. I think that is where he pulled himself up when he came out of the river. In those handprints, I saw his desperation. But because he had made them as he pulled himself UP, I saw hope on the hood of his car.

I tried to picture what it would have been like for him. I realize now I don't have to know how it felt or what it looked like or the minute-to-minute details. All I need to know is that he is here with us, and working every day to stay healthy. The river did not win that day and neither did depression. My uncle fought on the battlefield of his mental health anguish—and he came out victorious! I am immensely proud to be his niece. To this day, I still think about the hope in those handprints. I hope his story can help others find hope in their lives.

SIX WEEKS – MY FATHER AND FORGIVENESS

I very quickly discovered that being in hospital was a safe space for me. I also began to see that there was potential for change ... finally! In a little over a month, I had made three significant life decisions. The first was that I was going to leave this world immediately after the 50th birthday event. The second—and most important decision—I made while in the middle of the river was that I wanted to live. The third was that I would cease to try solving my problems just by myself, and to be open to anything and everything that could help me.

From the moment that Jan stated that we were going to the hospital, I started my recovery. At the hospital, I began the first stage of this journey—a six-week stay supervised by professionals 24/7. I was determined; I really wanted to get out of the deep dark hole that I was stuck in.

My first meeting with the resident psychologist happened at the end of my first week in the hospital. Since I decided to open myself up, I had to trust that this particular psychologist could help me. I told him both about my business partner's addictions and the subsequent stress his behaviours created on our business success as well as the many significant experiences of my childhood—all that led to my slide into deep depression.

It was only after I attempted suicide at age 50 and while I was in the hospital making every effort to rebuild myself that I could actually see depression symptoms in other people. In 2002, no one wanted to think about or talk about having depression, or a family member having depression. When a family member is hospitalized for mental illness, other family members can ignore and deny the diagnosis or they can support and acknowledge the difficult learning ahead for their loved one. I learned that sometimes the inability of a family member to visit and support a loved one through an illness like depression has nothing to do with the sick person, and everything to do with the emotional capacity of the family member.

When I went into the hospital, my sister Susan came to visit. Our discussion eventually led to Susan's observation that we were raised by an alcoholic father and a very controlling mother. We had indirectly talked about our parents' behaviours in the past, but never so bluntly. Our discussion gave me license to see it and believe it, providing me awareness to add to my healing. I began to think about events in my past … why did some things happen and why did I react as I did? My sister helped bring our negative family traits out in the open. I am a natural optimist and my optimism for healing grew with understanding my behaviours and those of my family members.

I can't begin to imagine what it would have been like for my parents and my sisters to know I was in the hospital because I tried to end my life. For them to accept what I was going through, they would have to find a way to recognize their own possible mental health challenges. They had to find a way to support me in a way that worked for them.

My depression and suicide attempt had a noticeably profound effect on my dad. He came to visit me almost every day. He showed immense growth as a person during my stay in hospital. My dad started talking to me about things he had done that had damaged me and he began apologizing—and kept on apologizing. That's the best therapy I could have received after being raised by someone whose words and actions had done harm to me. I admire him tremendously for taking on difficult life lessons at his age (77 at the time). He was always a very inquisitive person so it shouldn't have been a surprise that he began to look inward at himself and started analyzing things that had happened in the past.

My father's father was a known taskmaster who would take a swipe in anger at his boys from time to time. So, it is no surprise, my dad did the same to me. During his self-examination, he probably thought about how he felt about his father's abusive behaviour—then he began to have an understanding of what it had been like for me. We even talked about the deep dark secret of his father's suicide, and I learned more about the lasting impact of this deep dark secret on my dad.

My dad had been raised Catholic. After my grandfather suicided, the Catholic church refused to bury him in the Catholic All Saints Cemetery where he had purchased the family plot and buried his first wife and oldest son. Therefore, my grandfather was buried in Elmwood Cemetery, the public graveyard. As a result, my dad left the Catholic Church, and the family became members of the United Church. The cause of why my father left the Catholic Church was always there in the dark recesses of my mind.

Many years later, in 2012, a conversation between myself and a Catholic priest turned out to be fortuitous. Over coffee, our conversation shifted to my grandfather.

"I don't understand why a religious organization that believes in compassion would turn its back on a family at a time when it truly needed help, compassion and understanding," I said.

"John, would you like to move your grandfather to All Saints Cemetery?"

I was taken aback! Never had I considered this as an option.

With the kindness and help of others in the Catholic Church, I engineered the move of my grandfather's remains. Finally, he could rest with his family. My dad had suppressed his Catholic faith for so many years, neither going to Mass nor taking Communion in the Catholic church. Only after my grandfather's remains were moved did my dad feel free to became a practicing Catholic once again. His burden was finally lifted.

My dad was one of the many who joined together to obtain a grant from the Government of Canada to restore the Catholic church building in Meleb. Now designated as a heritage site, there is a plaque on one of the church walls stating the land was donated by Stefan and Paulina Melnick. My grandparents had homesteaded at what became Meleb in Manitoba. The town name is a combination of our surname Melnick and the surname of the Liebman family as both families had donated land for the church, school, and railway siding.

Once a year in the summer, the church has a Mass in order to maintain its status as a church. We had a family reunion in August 2015 and all attended the Mass. For the first time since my grandfather's death, my dad took Communion. He considered that act as a reaffirmation of his Catholic faith. He was in his nineties.

He died a few months later in October. My dad experienced a full circle—from his own troubled experiences with his father, to his experiences with his only son, to his own reconciliation and peace.

My dad and I did a lot of healing together. I am confident that he was able to find peace with his father's suicide. I know that he found peace with his son's attempt at suicide. We took the time. We talked. We listened. We healed together.

If we had talked about my grandfather's suicide earlier, maybe I would have been more aware of the signs of depression in myself. Depression or suicide in my family background was a clue that I was predisposed to mental illness. If I had been aware of this history, I could have taken action to protect myself.

If you have depression in your family background, start learning about depression right away.

RISE ABOVE

SIX WEEKS – FORGIVING MY MOTHER

One night when I was going to sleep in the hospital, I looked up and said to my greater power, "Tell me what I am supposed to do in order to heal."

In the morning, the answer was clear in my mind as to what I needed to do to move forward. First, I needed to identify the toxic people and unhealthy environments in my life, as their effect on me was poisonous and debilitating.

I had started to see the ward psychologist. He would ask the questions and I would search for the answers. I didn't try to hide any feelings or thoughts. I decided to just let everything tumble out. Names and faces and anger emerged—and one of those faces was my mother's.

During my six weeks in the hospital, my mother only came to see me once—about a week after I was admitted. I remember her arriving at the psychiatric ward, dressed like she was going to an important social event. I was still confused and disoriented, trying to get a handle on what had happened. I only remember one thing about our conversation during her visit. She wondered if I could tell her why I would do such a thing. I don't remember how I responded.

I was disappointed that she did not return. Her unwillingness to visit me could have been just her way of coping with my depression. Or maybe she wasn't willing to consider any responsibility in how her words and actions had affected my mental health.

I am not aware of my mother ever talking to anyone about me being in hospital. I wonder if she was frightened about what others would say to her or behind her back if they found out about my mental health struggles. Perhaps her absence was her response to the fact that she was not in control, a loss that would inspire in her both fear and panic. She couldn't control the agenda, nor the players. This was about me and she couldn't control the narrative or focus.

My mother always had to be the center of attention, even when other family members should have been the focus. She had always been very manipulative, twisting the words and intentions of others to suit her purposes and consistently changing her word as she desired to put her in the centre of attention.

My oldest sister was married when she was 19. She lived in Europe for a few years and when she would come back home for a visit, she would tell us that she wanted to just see her immediate family—to spend quality time with us. Although my mother might have initially acquiesced to my sister's request for a quieter visit, she would quickly change her mind and throw a large party. My mother ignored my sister's preference to the point where my sister simply stopped coming home.

My mother's twin brother Fred experienced the same thing when he would visit from British Columbia. My mother would put on a show, wonderful food would be prepared, and the place would be all clean and tidy. If there was a dinner, my mother would place name cards around the table, determining where each person would sit, thereby controlling who talked to whom. Uncle Fred was my favourite uncle and I was disappointed that he stopped coming to Winnipeg in an effort to avoid my mother's manipulations.

What angered me and my siblings was that mother heard us, but did not listen to us. Instead, she determined everyone's schedule to suit her. My Uncle Fred told me and my sisters that my mother had been that way since she was a little girl.

In 2011, after an absence of more than twenty years and knowing that his time was getting short, Uncle Fred, now 84 years old, emailed me that he wanted to come to Winnipeg one last time. He told me that he and Aunt Hazel just wanted to visit with a few people. I showed the email to my mother and she said she understood Uncle Fred's wishes. One week later, my mother called me. She told me she had spoken with Uncle Fred and that he had changed his mind and wanted to see as many relatives as possible. This was false. She wanted a big get-together and she was determined to have one.

This was standard operating procedure for my mother—bulldozing through with her own agenda regardless of the desires of others. She defended her actions with lies, claiming that the visiting relatives changed their minds about how many people they wanted to see.

I think that my dad just acquiesced, going along with my mother on what she wanted in these situations. He had placed her on a pedestal and she "ruled the roost". She was going to do what she wanted to do, no matter what anyone else wanted. Like all couples, my parents argued and more so when he stood up to her. After my mother died, I jokingly asked him whom he would argue with now that mother had gone. He replied that he didn't want to argue with anyone.

Until my swim into the river, I put up with my mother's behavior and I accepted the same inappropriate behaviour from others in my life. But then I changed. Even though it was not easy, I had to change in order to survive. After I swam into the river, my suppressed anger and frustration was released. I realized that my mother had trained my sisters and me to hold the anger inside, conditioning us to accept similar behaviour from others.

But now I stood up to my mother. In regards to Uncle Fred's visit, I sent an email to my sisters with a copy to my mother saying that I was not going to participate in any large gathering. My mother backed down this time, but she was not happy to do so. When Uncle Fred and Aunt Hazel did arrive in Winnipeg, they had a small visit with only my parents, my sister, and myself. It showed me that I had the strength to stand up to people who tried to control my life. My uncle told me that it was the best family visit he had ever had in Winnipeg.

When I was a child, the constant parties were an issue for my sisters and me because we felt we were growing up in a fish bowl. I look back and recall that if we ever challenged my mother, she would flip it around on us to make it seem as if we were the ones in the wrong. She controlled the information she shared about our family with neighbours and other relatives, regardless of whether we were bothered by the breach of privacy. One of my aunts told me that my mother lived her life through her children, which on the surface sounds endearing; however, as we moved into adulthood, we realized that her push for control would continue.

I learned to deal with my anger and then frustration regarding my mother through journaling and talking with the psychologist. The psychologist helped me through the stages. I read books to help me heal. One of those books was by Matthew McKay. The title, *When Anger Hurts,* alone told me that I was not alone in trying to deal with anger and hurt; it was tremendously comforting to know that others go through the same things.

I also learned to set new boundaries with others, especially my mother. It was a watershed moment when I set the boundary that I would not go along with a big party for Uncle Fred's visit.

Once I got past the anger, forgiveness followed. I learned that forgiveness can be a powerful act. One of my colleagues belonged to the same community as Helen Betty Osborne, a young Indigenous woman whose murder took seventeen years to solve. While the murderer was in prison, Elders from Helen's community went to see him. They forgave him! I couldn't believe that they would do that.

When I asked my colleague about this act of forgiveness,

she replied, "John, it's important for you to know that forgiveness frees you—and the Elders freed our community."

What a wonderful message to receive and learn. The phrase "The acid of anger can destroy the vessel it is kept in" is a great metaphor. I was at a point in my life that my mother no longer had control over me. I had established boundaries. Then came the forgiveness. When I forgave her in my own mind, it freed me. I believe that's how many people get past their anger.

A few months prior to my mother's passing, my sister Pauline, my dad and I had a lovely dinner at my parents' home. My mom's health was failing and we all knew she would not be with us much longer.

In a quiet voice, she said, "I never wanted to hurt any of you. I hope that those I did hurt will forgive me."

We all did. It was a freeing moment for us all.

Forgiveness does not mean continuing to take unhealthy or abusive behaviour. If someone is not going to change, we can release ourselves from obligation. Forgiveness gives us the ability to put distance between ourselves and past hurts and walk away with freedom and peace.

MOVING ON – COUNTING THE GOOD THINGS

Talking and learning about myself, my family dynamics and my depression were key elements to healing. Another major component was medication. Unfortunately, discovering the best medication and the most appropriate dosage was not an easy task. During the early weeks in the hospital, I was frustrated about the lack of progress in finding the right medication and quantity. About halfway through my stay in hospital, the psychiatrist tried a new combination of medications. It worked and my mood started to get lighter.

I was on the path to repairing the relationship with my father and understanding and forgiving my mother, but there were other relationships I needed to address as well. I had learned after waking up with that crystal clarity that I needed to identify toxic people and unhealthy environments, but I also needed to install boundaries in other relationships where people were taking far more than they were giving. This would require walking away from a successful business that I had worked so hard to grow.

After I became a group insurance salesperson in 1980, I was promoted to become the manager of the Saskatoon office. On top of that leadership role, I still hit amazing sales numbers considering the size of the community I served; placing third in the country when my competitors were from Toronto, Montreal and Vancouver set me on a firm path of success in my industry. I moved from Saskatoon back to Manitoba, where in the Winnipeg group sales office, I posted the highest sales numbers to date in that agency. I transferred into the Winnipeg individual sales office where I set a record for high sales results. I became licensed to sell mutual funds and won numerous sales contests in that area.

You would think with this level of career success, I would not be experiencing any low feelings, depression or sadness. However, I did. Many people think depression is an emotion (rather than a condition) that can be remedied by just being more successful. But my workplace relationship with my business partner had become untenable. I needed to walk away from my business partnership—which had become the main source of my re-emergence of depression.

The last strategy I had awoken with was to recognize the good things that I had going for me.

The list of good things started with my loving wife. Jan came to see me every day in the hospital. On her first visit, she was fiery and determined.

"John, I am here for you. We're going to get through this," she insisted. Jan brought all she had: love, pharmaceutical training, inquisitiveness, and most of all, a resolve to never give up. I found out how truly amazing this woman is. I am so glad I married her.

Secondly, was my financial situation. Thanks to my disability plan, which paid my monthly expenses, we had our financial security needs met. This was a good thing. Since our base needs of food and shelter were protected, I was free to process what had happened. Upon reflection, I was able to clearly see the impact of my negative business relationship. It was easier to realize the negative impact now that I had removed myself from the unhealthy business situation and work environment.

The third good thing I focused on was positive relationships. I had loving family members and caring friends, all who expressed sincere wishes that I improve. Instead of offering unsolicited advice, they asked me, "John, what do you need from me to help you get through this?" This was exactly the kind of support I needed. Recovery from depression should be led by the person afflicted by the depression. They know what they need.

Next came my own resolve. I was determined to move forward.

Finally, of course, was baseball.

I found it ironic that the World Series took place during my six weeks in the psychiatric ward. The timing couldn't have been any better because it was a west coast World Series, the LA Angels versus the Oakland As. The Angels won, which was a first for a wild card team. They were underdogs and I was inspired that they were victorious. On the psychiatric ward, we were supposed to be in bed by 10:15 p.m., but I convinced the nurses that baseball was better medication for me than anything else. Each evening, I watched the game in the TV lounge, getting back to my room around midnight. I would fall asleep analyzing the game.

Baseball feeds my soul and it fed my healing. Sometimes, my inner John the Jokester would wonder—somewhere in the back of my subconscious mind—did I time the walk into the river so my stay in hospital would take place during the World Series?

Just before I was discharged, a very special psychiatric nurse reminded me of two important things to take away with me to enhance my journey to wellness. "John, you have to develop a plan for recovery. You can control your mental health issues and you can control your mental health illness. But you need to have a plan to help you succeed in both."

Those words really impacted me and stay with me to this day. As a reminder to always be positive, I got a tattoo at the front of my right shoulder, *carpe diem*, Latin for "seize the day". In the morning after my shower, I see it in the mirror and I say to myself, "Carpe diem" and think about at least one positive action I will do that day.

Then she urged, "And secondly, get toxic people out of your life and be with people who support you and are good for you to be around."

Those two ideas became the foundation that I developed all my other tools and processes around to maintain good balance and good mental health.

MOVING ON – DAILY REMINDERS OF SURVIVAL

On October 31, 2002, I was finally discharged after my six-weeks stay in the hospital. Piper was there to greet me at the front door like only dogs can—with his unconditional, enthusiastic and adoring happiness. His human was back!

Although I had wondered if I would be afraid to be away from the daily watch of mental health experts, this did not happen. I trusted my determination to become healthy. I reminded myself that I was moving forward into the next stage of my recovery.

I went upstairs to my bedroom and opened my sock drawer. On April 28, 2002, I had written a note about my mental health. It read, "My goal is to come out of depression." Then, four months later, on August 24th, I placed a newspaper article beneath the note about the Winnipeg Blue Bombers making an amazing comeback to beat the Calgary Stampeders.

Now home after my lengthy hospital stay, I looked at my note. So much had happened in the last six months. I saw the note and the newspaper article from a different perspective. When I wrote it, I knew my depression was bad. But staring at the note now, I felt hope and purpose.

Although the note was written before the river attack, I now see how it was my unconscious beginning of healing. The reason I chose the sock drawer was that I go into that sock drawer every day. So, I saw the note every day. I would have to touch it and move it aside to access my sock choice of the day. The fact that I had to touch it reminded me to read it.

Sometimes people put a note somewhere and it becomes just a part of the scenery. They forget the note and what's written upon it. That is why I put mine in a place where I had to touch it every day. Without consciously realizing it back in April, I had adopted one of my new cornerstone supports or strategies: **Choose to have hope and not give up.**

Although I now have a beard, back then, I was clean shaven. I could have put a note on top of my electric razor because I used it every day. I could have wrapped the note around my toothbrush; but my daily paper reminder would definitely not have been as durable so near a sink and water. I had looked for something that would keep me focused on this goal. Something accessible and in a secure place. The sock drawer logically won.

My *carpe diem* tattoo reminds me that I want to seize the day and live life to the fullest. *Carpe diem* is a Latin term that has stood the test of time. I first became aware of the Latin phrase watching the 1989 movie "Dead Poets Society." I was impressed with how it was used in the movie as a mantra for moving forward, being positive—and that's why I chose it for my tattoo.

Not only do I want to improve and focus on my own mental health, but I want to help others. When I trust people or think that message of the tattoo could help them, I pull my shirt aside and show them the tattoo. I tell them to seize the day, to do something good with it. This is another strategy that I fell into without realizing: *Find purpose and live that purpose!*

The final and most powerful strategy I incorporated is one of being inspired and taking action: *Rise Above!* Hardly a day goes by without me using this phrase, whether I use it to sign off on an email, while I am coaching individuals, or when at the front of a room speaking to a group. I try to inspire other people to improve their mental health or get past something they need to get past. When I am asked, "Rise above what?" I tell them whatever you need to get past. The phrase is open to anything and everything that people need to rise above.

These three strategies dealing with hope, purpose and inspiration gave me a good foundation to build on. I was working to heal in the best possible way I could. When I look back at my first day home, I knew how important it was for me to be solid in my strategies so I could someday encourage others to develop their own strategies for whatever challenges they would encounter in life.

Choose to have hope and not give up!
Find purpose and live that purpose!
Rise Above!

RISE ABOVE

MOVING ON – CORRECTING DYSFUNCTIONAL THOUGHT

What you think determines how you feel. How you feel determines how you act. Therefore, determining and understanding what you think and why you think it is vital. Cognitive Behavioural Therapy (CBT) is a very useful tool in achieving this awareness because it causes you to stop and analyze your thinking and ask whether your thoughts are really true or not.

When I say to others, "Rise Above," I am suggesting they come up with ideas that they think are workable—that they can plant in their mind. *First*, they need to be aware of what exactly they need to rise above and then they need to come up with a strategy as to how to rise above that particular challenge.

In other words: *You have a lot of power over what you think. Your thinking drives your emotions and your emotions drive your actions.*

William Shakespeare, in his Hamlet tragedy, wrote, "There is nothing either good or bad, but thinking makes it so." Therefore, if we as individuals think something is negative, we experience negative thoughts, followed by negative emotions, triggering negative actions. Conversely, if positive thoughts are attached to a situation, they drive positive emotions and positive actions.

Consider baseball players. If a pitcher throws a ball, and the batter hits a home run, the pitcher could become upset about that home run. Or the pitcher could think, "Thank God, I don't have to see that player for another eight batters and maybe not even for the remainder of the game." As a baseball pitcher for many years, I have found myself in that exact position. If I allowed myself to think I was a bad pitcher because of one home run, I emotionally felt down, and therefore it was no surprise that I performed poorly for the remainder of that game. However, in this same situation, if I put my mind in a positive mindset, my emotions stayed positive and so did the game's outcome. Although I had watched professional pitchers interviewed and learned from them the power of positive thinking, it wasn't until my six-week stay in hospital that I learned the science behind the power of changing my thoughts.

Analyzing your thoughts and applying CBT can be a good mental health process. When I was in the depths of depression, I found myself thinking that I added no value to the lives of others. Depression, as a condition, can often create in the individual a belief of low self value. Fighting back against negative thoughts is much more challenging when you are in a depressive state. Before I understood how important my mindset was, when a friend would say, "John, you're a good person," I wouldn't believe him if I was in a depressive state. But after understanding more about how my mind worked, when someone tells me I am a good person, by using the CBT process, I am able to change my thoughts and believe their message.

I can't imagine how different my life would have been if I had learned about CBT when I had my undiagnosed depression in my twenties. How would I have handled business stresses differently? I will never know. However, since learning about these vital strategies, I have incorporated them into my everyday life.

As a result of being hospitalized with clinical depression, I qualified to attend a ten-session program on improving your mental health using Cognitive Behavioural Therapy (CBT). About a month after my release from hospital, I enrolled in the course. A few lessons into the program, I was introduced to the Dysfunctional Thought Record. This strategy helped me to identify and change negative thoughts into positive ones.

I learned that we all have cognitive distortions or traps that we fall into. Learning about cognitive distortions really helped me to free myself and unhook myself from negative thoughts, feelings and actions. Whenever my mood is deteriorating, I create a dysfunctional thought record. I ask myself, "What's going on in my mind right now?" and chart the following information:

- Date and time
- Situation
- Initial thoughts
- Initial emotions
- Initial outcome
- Alternative thoughts
- Alternative emotions
- Alternative outcome

For example, let's go back to the example of the baseball pitcher.

(Situation) In the middle of a high-pressure game, the batter hits a home run.
(Initial thoughts) The pitcher might think: "I am a bad pitcher."
(Initial emotions) low self-worth, anger, and frustration
(Initial outcome) poor performance

An alternative response could be:

(Alternative thought) "I'll get him out next time he's up to the plate."
(Alternative emotion) motivation
(Alternative outcome) positive performance and a desire to try harder in the future.

I began to see where my thought process would pull me down. At first it was hard to be objective and look at alternate responses. After a while, the process became easier and I could change my negative thoughts quicker. This process really worked. I was adjusting to thinking and living differently.

TIME TO RE-EXAMINE
TIME MANAGEMENT

Up to 1997, I had a good balance of how I spent my time. Then I started getting pulled more and more into the business and the schedules and projects of others. I have always wanted to accommodate the needs of others and rarely say no. I just found a way to fit their request into my schedule.

Not only that, the nature of my business work changed and became more time intensive. My time balance had become lopsided, with all the attention focused on chasing the wrong tasks. I had not taken a regular holiday for more than five years. My hours were increasing almost every week, first to 50 and gradually to more than 60.

As all this was happening, my depression was coming on. That made it harder to work longer hours. The inability to sleep well or sleep long are side effects of depression and my sleep deficit made it harder and harder to keep up with my work.

During my time in hospital, I didn't have to do any work—except work on myself. Although I certainly wouldn't classify it as a holiday, it forced me into down time, business-wise.

Before I walked into the river, I thought that I was reasonably good at time management. But I was only good at time management when things were going well. As I healed and learned about depression and about myself, I realized that the element I was missing in my time management practices was not knowing how to step back and adjust. I know without a doubt that had I known what I know now, my depression would not have pulled me in to the extent that I walked into the river.

I didn't know how to deal with overload. I didn't know how to say, "No." I would say, "Yes" to too many people. I eventually learned that good time management is essential to good mental health, particularly because good time management leads to reduced stress regarding deadlines. I began to say, "No" to some requests for help and began to tell people I would do a task, but only with a deadline that was realistic for me.

After my time in hospital, I gradually adopted practices that I honed over time.

1) Prioritize my projects
2) Reprioritize my projects when one project is taking more time than I first planned
3) Reprioritize when a new project appears
4) Do a gut check on how comfortable and satisfied I am on where I spend my time.

For example, when a respected aunt passed away in 2003, I was her Executor of her estate. I put other projects on hold while I dealt with her estate issues as this was a new project and required me to reprioritize what projects I currently was working on and the timelines within which they would be completed.

After I adopted these practices, I began to track my time and constantly review my daily calendar. When something new comes in, I look at my schedule. Then I rank everything by order of importance. I look at how many hours I want to work in the day, and look at the numbers of hours each project will need. Then when I reach my maximum hours I wish to work, I put the incomplete work aside.

I work hard at mastering this process. After twenty years of reviewing and adjusting my workload and prioritizing my schedule, it is a well-ingrained process that has enabled me to be successful with projects while maintaining good care of my mental and physical health. This ensures that I don't get into time pressures, which can lead to tiredness and eventually depression.

For example, in June 2020, I began working on a *Singing for Peace* fundraising concert to be performed in September. Towards the end of July, I started to realize that there was a lot more work involved than I had originally thought. This awareness triggered a reprioritizing. In the old days, I would have just plowed through. Now, I reprioritized.

I was just starting to write my story around the time the concert planning began. I initially thought that I could handle both along with other activities. Then I realized that this wasn't possible without a cost—to my mental and physical health as well as to the quality of my work. Again, time to stop, evaluate, reprioritize.

During the business years leading up to my depression, I was overloaded. I didn't set boundaries for how much work I would or could do. I just kept accepting more projects and saying "Yes" to too many people.

I often think about the song *Cat's in the Cradle* by Harry Chapin when I work on time management. The singer describes how he had a son, but he was too busy to spend much time with his child in his growing up years. There were planes to catch, and bills to pay and he promised his son that when he came home, they would spend time together but they never did. The boy grows up and when he comes home from college, the father asks him to sit for a while but he says he didn't have time. The boy moves away and the father calls and asks for him to visit, but the son says, "I'd love to, Dad, if I could find the time. You see, my new job's a hassle, and the kids have the flu. But it's sure nice talking to you, Dad. It's been sure nice talking to you." And the father replies to himself, "As I hung up the phone, it occurred to me, he'd grown up just like me."

Any parent can understand how easy it is to be bogged down with work and families suffer as a result. Tracking time and seeing where it's going is vital. If important activities like spending time with your children are not happening, you can adjust and control your time going forward.

Proper time management practices help us to maintain balance and quality of life which then helps us to maintain good mental health. People often think about time management in an effort to increase their productivity, but rarely in terms of mental health.

So how do I decide if I have good time management skills?

First, look back at your appointment book for the past several weeks. If you don't keep an appointment book, start a time log and record your activities so you can analyze your time usage.

As well as recording your activities and time spent on each, ask yourself questions like:

Did I estimate the correct amount of time to do the task?

Over time, I've learned how to predict how much time it takes me to do something. I applied what I've learned to the *Singing for Peace* project. I was chairing the project and could see that it was taking a great deal of my time, so I moved a few things (including my book project) to after the concert was over. I knew that continuing with my current projects and chairing the concert would have been exhausting. Before my hospital stay, I would have tried to keep everything going without regard to the toll that it would take on me, or the quality of my work. Between that recognition and understanding how to apply time management techniques, I put my mental and physical health first.

I consider the *Singing for Peace* project and how I dealt with my time a learned success.

How does time management connect to mental health? By delaying a few projects, I ensured that I was not cutting out time with Jan while I worked on various projects. Leading up to my River Attack, the deeper I immersed myself in my work, the less time I spent with Jan. Now, in my scheduling, I prioritize spending time with Jan. Nothing is more important than this.

A vital part of my time management planning includes significant time for sleep. When I look back at those years in business when I worked all the time, I was often exhausted and sleeping poorly. At the time, I just didn't think about needing sleep. There was always too much work to do and too many things swirling around in my mind. I would work Sundays, evenings. When markets go down, clients need assurance that things are going to work out over time. This requires many hours over the phone to calm their nerves. I was knowledgeable about the ups and downs of the market and wanted to provide good service to my clients. Soon, I was working more than 60 hours a week. I felt I was on a never-stopping treadmill.

What do you do with your time? Do you need to shift where and how you spend it?

Sometimes a journey naturally comes to an end and sometimes you must make the decision to end a journey. As I assessed how I was spending time, I realized that I needed a change regarding my participation in one of my service clubs. As I looked forward to the future and the projects and issues that were dear to my heart, I realized that my focus was not in alignment with my current club, and I needed to find one that was. I had discovered that when I contributed to issues that were important to me, I was positively affecting my mental health. I didn't want to leave the organization, I only wanted to shift to a club that met my desire to contribute to my city and country in a way that made sense to me.

I really enjoyed my years in the service club and felt great reward as one does from participating in an organization that exists to help the local community. However, I trusted my process and the result was that the change worked for me. I certainly had trepidation (I was after all changing a 30-year habit) but sometimes change brings renewed energy and once I made the decision and took the proverbial plunge, it worked. My decision gave me renewed purpose as I found myself surrounded by like-minded volunteers.

Sometimes we reach the end of our rope and are so overwhelmed that we want to throw in the towel and quit, even if the situation is one we valued being part of in the past. I took a risk of making a change instead of leaving the organization. Sometimes we can make a pivot and decide to use our time in a better, healthier way without throwing away the enjoyment and sense of contribution.

Or we can try something different, something new. If you are in an unhealthy job situation, you do not have to stay in the job at all costs. It's okay if you need to leave for the sake of your mental health and well-being. If you leave yourself open to go in a new direction, then you can discover all kinds of new things.

RISE ABOVE

PLANNING FOR GOOD MENTAL HEALTH

Each evening during my six-week stay in the mental health ward in the fall of 2002, a psychiatric nurse would meet with me to find out how I was feeling. She would listen to my answers with great attention, and often gave me suggestions to consider to aid in my recovery. One night, she suggested, "You have to have a plan, the purpose of which will be to improve your mental health." I took that advice to heart and started that night to develop my plan.

I will forever be indebted to the mental health team that helped get me through those first six weeks of my recovery. The next stage put me back into my regular environment. I have learned to talk about how I got into that deep dark hole but more importantly how I got out of it. My collection of tools and strategies (the plan my nurse encouraged me to develop) was at a basic stage when I left the hospital, but I continued to grow and develop. Perhaps others who wish to improve their mental health will find some helpful ideas in this collection.

Make it personal

It is important that we make the strategies that we choose to adopt personal. For example, no one needs to know about a note that I wrote and put in my sock drawer but I know it's there. I touch it and read the words: *My goal is to come out of my depression. I think about what I can do today to help me avoid depression.* It's the same with my tattoo. No one needs to know about it but I know it's there. I make a point of repeating what it says every morning: *Carpe diem.* Seize the day. Do something positive today.

Find a mantra

"Rise Above!" has become my mantra, my call to action for using good healthy thinking. If no one reacts to it, that's okay. I use it to help me stay positive regardless of what others think.

Journal

I record things that are going on in my life and how I am feeling about them. This way I can recognize things which pull me down and figure out how to deal with them. I make entries usually on a daily basis, and especially when I start to experience a change in my mood. Looking back over weeks, months, and now years, I can see patterns. For example, I often go into a "down mood" after Christmas and it often lasts until early March. So, I do not take on many projects at that time. Deadlines and heavy workloads associated with projects add stress, which can lead to loss of sleep. That, in turn, can lead to anxiety and push me into depression. I realized that January to March is a high-risk time for me when I saw the pattern in my journal.

When I look back to my early twenties, I believe now that I experienced undiagnosed depression. I used the technique of journaling to self-heal my depression during my trip to Europe by writing in a diary about what makes life good. Although I didn't realize it at the time, I had engaged in my own version of talk therapy, eventually un-trapping myself.

Have daily routines

There was a tree in my back yard that got sick when I did. We bought nutrient sticks and stuck them in the ground under the tree. We nursed it back to health and it became a symbol of recovery for me. It healed along with me. I called it the *Recovery Tree* and I found it calming to spend time in its company.

Have evening routines

Routine is important because it helps to normalize processes. Even your routines before bed. I take my medication at the same time every night. Then I go to my big comfy chair (which I named Big Brown) and I write the day's highs and lows in my journal. I keep the journal as a means of recording my moods and what was happening when I felt up or down. Then I check email and do an online crossword puzzle. This pre-bed routine does what it is supposed to do. It makes me sleepy. Most importantly, it helps me focus on getting regular sleep. When I first got sick in 2002, I was sleeping less than one hour a night. My evening routine and properly adjusted medications shift me from craving sleep to getting restful sleep.

Gather your team

Everyone's depression is different. Environment or events can trigger your depression, or you may be predisposed to depression if there is a family history. It is very important to recognize that if you've had depression once, chances are that you will get it again. That's why developing a relationship with a team of doctors is so critical. So many people give up if a treatment doesn't work. Just like pedaling a bike, you just have to keep going. When something doesn't work, try something else. Keep trying until you find something that does work.

I am the Co-ordinator of my medical team that I have gathered around me. My general practitioner monitors my overall health. He keeps an eye on blood pressure, sugar levels, weight and things necessary for good physical health. My psychologist, whom I have been seeing since 2002, monitors my moods and helps me find ways to live healthier from a mental health perspective. My psychiatrist monitors my medications, which may be adjusted from time to time. My role as the coordinator is to meet with each one regularly and advise each one what the other two are doing or what has been recommended. Keeping all three informed is key. It is easier to treat a patient when you have the whole picture.

Find Activities to Give Your Mind a Health Break

I love baseball and when I go to the ballpark to watch a game, time ceases to exist. The sights, sounds, and smells of the ballpark take over my senses, which I welcome. For about three hours, I forget about everything else. Occasionally, I keep score throughout the innings and then I am completely involved in the game. It is a labor of love. I recently spoke to a woman who loves to dance the tango. Going to a dance class and dancing has the same effect on her as baseball has on me.

But don't just sit in the stands. Make sure to include physical activity in your daily routine. Choose something you like *doing because you are more likely to keep doing it*. Exercise is related to positive mental health and it may provide relief in symptoms of depression and anxiety.

Use Cognitive Behavioral Therapy

In an earlier chapter, I wrote about Cognitive Behavioral Therapy or CBT. I have taken two courses in this process. The premise of the therapy is that we base our actions on emotions and base our emotions on thoughts. If we are not thinking clearly, we find ourselves in a negative tangle of destructive thoughts, not based on reality, but based on "twisted thinking." CBT can teach us to check our thoughts, thus preventing us from getting into negative mindsets based on conclusions arrived at through erroneous assumptions, and I apply these techniques on a daily basis.

Keep Personal Relationships Healthy

It is important to foster healthy relationships. Many relationships start out on a healthy basis, but over time can become toxic. When this happens, boundaries might have to be set or re-established. In some cases, terminating the relationship is the only healthy choice. I developed an acronym for my process of identifying and building healthy relationships – I call it STARS.

(S) Sincere - Both persons must be sincere about the friendship and desire good outcomes for each other.

(T) Truthful - You are truthful with each other. You do not "sugar coat" things. I would rather my friends be truthful, even if it initially hurts to hear what they say. The best way to grow is to hear the truth. Then you are dealing with reality—and dealing with reality is critical to good mental health.

(A) Acrobatic - The relationship must be able to climb and leap over hurdles, especially unforeseen, significant ones. Since my depression in 2002, I have become a very different person and not everyone can handle my new straightforward approach. My healthy relationships continue, as we work together *acrobatically*, leaping hurdles as they come our way.

(R) Resilient - Relationships ebb and flow. The best ones are resilient and can bounce back. When you run into a problem or conflict, discuss it, resolve it, and move on.

(S) Silly - With true friends you can be silly. Joking is tremendously healthy, so encourage each other to be silly more often. It has a way of lightening things up and releasing healthy endorphins into your system to make you feel happy and relaxed.

OWNING WHAT USED TO OWN ME

Sharing my story with others who I know are experiencing depression is one way to see the value in my experience. This wasn't my idea, but my cousin Roberta's, who also struggles with depression. On September 19th, 2002, I went into hospital and I received her letter on the 29th – ten days later. This is what she wrote:

Hey, John,

Long time, no talk.

My mom told me of your battle with depression and I thought maybe you might like or need someone in a similar "fight" to just listen.

You see, since the birth of my almost five-year-old son, I have been stricken with depression. My worst days were about two years ago.

Yes, it was ugly. I bought eight bottles of sleeping pills in front of my children. I had a plan of how and when to complete my task so as to not inconvenience my loved ones too much.

I don't know why I didn't follow through. Lack of courage … I guess.

I am not healed by any means, but I have considered my outlook stable for about a good year. I have tried three different antidepressants, but with no luck.

I have begun journaling, as I have admitted to myself, my "issues" are eating me alive. I have so many—it seems to me anyways—that I was confused as to where and how to begin dealing with them.

Anyhow, I did not write this to you to pour my heart out, or make you feel responsible for me in any way. My intention in writing to you is to let you know that I am here to chat with, help, sort out, or just listen and empathize.

I do not expect anything of you, John. If you choose not to get involved in that way with me, that's fine. No pressure. If now is not a good time and ten years from now is—my offer does not expire.

I do hope that your road of healing has begun, or will shortly. It will be hell, I am sure. No beating around the bush here. If you're concerned with the pain and guilt you might inflict on those whom you have issues with, trust that they are strong enough to bear it. Apparently, you have shouldered all too much crap for far too long and need to drop some of that load.

Best of luck John and may you find comfort with your life.

Your cousin, Roberta

A few years into my recovery, after I began to speak publicly on the topic of mental health, I received an email from Roberta. She commented on how far I had come in my path towards good mental health and said, *"You now own what used to own you."* She knew that my depression had been in control of my life but that now I was the one in control.

When I first spoke at my service club after my time in the hospital, I spoke about my depression and about what I had learned. I spoke about the stigma surrounding mental health and how it impedes people from searching out and getting solutions to their mental health issues. I encouraged people to talk to their doctors about mental health.

In the following months, people began to approach me about my presentation. I was surprised at how many reached out to me who were not members of my service club, or didn't even hear my presentation in person. At the time, no one was comfortable to speak openly, but it was a good first step that they contacted me privately and I was happy to talk to anyone who contacted me. I was surprised at how appreciative they were and a few even told me that they talked to their doctors and experienced improvement in their lives. As more people contacted me, I could start to see my role helping people on a larger scale. If others saw that I was comfortable talking about my depression, then maybe it might inspire them to talk openly as well.

I was amazed at the pass-it-forward possibilities. I saw that perhaps by talking about my experiences and showing where I am today, I could give others hope. What better purpose is there than to demonstrate by example that we can live with depression and have good lives. That first presentation in my service club was a start. I wanted to continue finding ways to help people. In that first year after my September 2002 River Attack, not only could I talk to people about my experiences, I could help direct them to the resources available to those who need help, starting with their family doctor.

One of my colleagues called me a ground breaker because I was male, over fifty, and baring my soul for the benefit of helping others. I proudly accepted his label for me.

In owning what used to own me, and in my goal to reaching others in their own mental health challenges, I can reflect on the following lessons:

Lesson: After a significant event, be self-aware and pay attention to loved ones.

Thomas Holmes and Richard Rahe developed the Holmes Rahe Stress Scale as a way to determine whether stressful events might cause illnesses. They tested the validity of the stress scale as a predictor of illnesses and found a positive correlation between life events and the illnesses.

One significant event alone can easily cause stress and anxiety. Have you ever lost a spouse or close relative? Have you lost a job and your sole source of income? Were you seriously injured or diagnosed with a life-threatening illness? These are just a few significant events. Be self-aware and watch for changes in you, your friends, colleagues and loved ones.

Lesson: Look in your family tree for clues as to where you might be headed.

Regarding physical illnesses, such as cancer, we are all encouraged to check and see if there is a history of the condition in our family. And if there is, we are advised to take steps to protect ourselves when possible. If I had reflected on the mental health issues in my family history, I might have realized that I was heading in a direction that might be repeating family history. It wouldn't be unexpected for me to have depression.

So, I tell people:

There is an old expression: *forewarned is forearmed*. It means if you know something in advance, you can be prepared. Consider the profound value of the two above lessons and how powerful those simple approaches could be in approaching and preventing the onset of depression.

Lesson: Talk about mental health.

When I shared my story for the first time, I realized what a positive domino effect speaking out about my mental health could have. I did something very simple and people listened.

But how do you talk about mental health? Put yourself in a situation where you have experienced significant stress and anxiety and your loved ones saw what was happening.

Did your loved ones do anything?
Did they not know what to do?
Did they have the toolset to know what to do?

In the case of my depression that led to my River Attack in 2002, the answers to the three questions above were no. None of my family members—my wife, my sisters, and my parents—knew what depression was all about. My wife felt helpless and powerless. She saw something wasn't right but she didn't know what to do. She would today.

Since my recovery, my wife has been my strongest ally in terms of when she sees me moving towards unhappiness or undue anger. She will mention it. One of the first things I will do is sit back. I will cut back appointments, move things off my plate to a later date. Or just get out of them altogether. She knows what to do now.

**Lesson: Depression can come in waves,
grabbing, releasing, grabbing, releasing.**

Now looking back, there were times when the depression was stronger but then it would ease. It would come back stronger, and then it would ease again. I would be happy, buoyant, like I usually am. They would think, *oh, he's feeling better.* They wouldn't know that my depression was still there. My pattern is that I stop doing everything in a depressed state. When I returned from Europe and got back into the same social circle, my friends commented that they were glad to see me back. They put my new state of ease down to my time away. They didn't see my struggle to return to the state of ease. They didn't know what happened because they didn't see all of my experience.

Imagine living with the grab and release. Even today, it is still there *inside* me—like the ebb and flow of water.

Lesson: Learn to live the good life

Part of my plan for conquering my depression was to Live the Good Life and that meant staying away from toxic people and gravitating toward people whom I can work with.

I used to take on a project, then another one, then another one, eventually working myself into exhaustion. Now, I'm strict with my routine, and I constantly review the things that I have taken on and the things that I have committed to.

I've learned that exercise plays an important role in my mental as well as physical health. I go to a fitness centre about three times a week for about an hour. I do a combination of weights, walking the track and pedal on a bike. There is something very comforting about the repetitiveness of pedaling a bike. It's very meditative.

Now my routine is the same every evening and my sleep is regular and restful. The more routine I have, the better it is for my mental health. I like the regularity of the many good mental health processes I discovered and adopted. I like the routine of seeing my *Carpe Diem!* tattoo or picking up my note from the sock drawer. I recognize how much routine helps me.

I am happy every time I see people speaking publicly about mental health. We know we have made progress in the awareness of mental health issues because whenever a news announcer talks about someone who suicided, a banner is displayed along the bottom of the screen on where to go for help. The message, front and centre to the unfortunate news story, is that help is always available.

I went from being an award-winning entrepreneur to walking into a river. The tough guy image is not a healthy image where mental health is concerned. It isn't good to "suck it up and shut up." It is better to reach out and talk. Contact https://talksuicide.ca or call 1-833-456-4566 toll free.

LIFE GOES ON

As much as I want to help other individuals and need to work on my own mental health, I also want to do everything I can to break the occurrences of depression in my own family. From both sides of the family, I am a third-generation sufferer of serious depression.

I want to show future generations that we can live with depression and have good mental health. I have communicated with all my cousins and suggested that everyone learn about depression for their own good and for the sake of their children and future generations.

Armed with awareness, I hope my relatives will see the signs in their families but also in themselves. I hope that both within their immediate families and between generations, they create an environment where it's okay to talk about how they feel. I hope they have the courage to say when they're not okay. I hope that they know that it's okay to not be okay. Most importantly, I hope that future generations won't even know what it would be like to feel ashamed and hide their depression like an awful family secret.

Awareness is everything. Acceptance and support are of great value to someone living with depression. My strategies for living with depression have held since 2002. I continue to tweak as I learn new elements through my own experiences or through listening to and observing others.

Mental health is something that we all can talk about. Gestures, no matter how small, can make a difference to someone. Think about a smile or a compliment making someone's day. For someone dealing with depression, a simple gesture can become even more significant. I wasn't alone in my struggles with depression. The support that I received from all sources helped me to a place of healing and maintaining good mental health.

Reach out.
Talk about it.
Surround yourself with good people who will work with you and help you.
You are not alone.
Rise Above.

WHERE TO TURN?

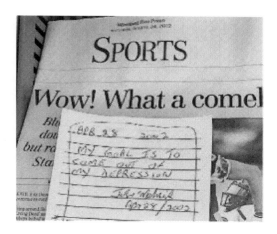

My friend, Norm Velnes came to see me shortly after I entered Victoria Hospital after my suicide attempt. Norm said, "There is not much in this world that cannot be fixed." And that is true. The first step is getting help.

You deserve to be heard – whether you are concerned about someone you care about or concerned about your own mental health and depression.

Talk Suicide Canada, is there to listen. Connect to a crisis responder to get help without judgement. Contact https://talksuicide.ca/

If you or someone you know is in immediate crisis or has suicide-related concerns, please call 1-833-456-4566 toll free.

RISE ABOVE

ABOUT THE AUTHOR

John Melnick was born in 1952 in Winnipeg, Manitoba, Canada. He has lived there all his life, except for the five years he spent in Saskatoon. During his time in Saskatchewan, from 1980 to 1985, he met the love of his life, Jan McGillivray. They have been married since 1987.

Always active in sports, John is in the Manitoba Baseball Hall of Fame and the Manitoba High School Sports Hall of Fame. In 1975, John graduated from the University of Manitoba with a Bachelor degree in Communications and a major in Business Math and spent the next 27 years in the Financial Services industry.

In 2002, John endured a severe clinical depression. On September 19th, 2002, he swam into the fast-flowing Red River, thinking that the only way to end the horrible pain of depression was to end his life. In the middle of the river, he decided to live. He swam back out and spent the next six weeks in the psychiatric ward of the Victoria Hospital.

John has been "in recovery" ever since.

In early 2003, he sold his Financial Planning practice and started searching for the cause of his depression and ways he could become mentally healthy. In "Rise Above," John shares what led to his depression and the strategies he has discovered to improve his own mental health. His hope is that the strategies in this book will be of benefit to others.

ACKNOWLEDGEMENTS

September 19th, 2002 was a huge watershed day for me. In the depths of a severe clinical depression, I swam into the fast-flowing Red River, thinking I could escape the worst pain I have ever experienced by ending my life. My desire to live prevailed—and I swam out, drove home, and was taken to the Victoria Hospital by my dear wife Jan. I have been in recovery ever since. This book would not have been possible without many people who have enlightened, empowered, and encouraged me since that day.

Thank you to my family:

Jan—your strength and willingness to help me learn about my illness is amazing.

My sisters—Pauline, Susan and Beverley—who shared with

---

me the events that happened to all of us in our youth in an effort to shed light on areas which I needed to be aware of.

My nieces—Rhonda, Cynthia, Mandi and Lisa—and my nephew Johann: you have been with me and supportive of me all along this journey.

Thank you to the three women who have helped make this book possible:

Jade Gritzfeld—for her collaborative editing work on the first edition of the manuscript.

Carlene Clark—thank you for your Social Media magic.

Jeanne Martinson at Wood Dragon Books—I am thankful for your expertise and compassion for my project. This book would never have been produced without you.

Thank you to the members of my clubs, especially:

Two Rotary Clubs (Winnipeg West and Winnipeg) – you have been truly helpful in the 35 years I have been a Rotarian.

Toastmasters Clubs—over the past 35 years, I have met so many great people and learned communication techniques which help me "get the word out" on the issue of mental health.

Breakfast Club—you are an astounding group of First Nations, Indigenous and Non-Indigenous people! 20 years of working with you has allowed me to learn so much about how to listen and learn and then speak.

TO CONTACT JOHN ...

To speak at your book club ...
To speak to your service club ...
To speak to your non-profit organization ...
To speak to your employees ...

Email: info@johnmelnick.ca
Website: www.JohnMelnick.ca

Manufactured by Amazon.ca
Bolton, ON

33306186R00070